Alaska Bound

Margaret Frank

Literary Wanderlust | Denver, Colorado

Published in the United States by Literary Wanderlust LLC, Denver, Colorado. www.LiteraryWanderlust.com

ISBN Print: 978-1-942856-47-4
ISBN eBook: 978-1-942856-53-5

Cover design: Pozu Mitsuma

Printed in the United States

Dedication

For my mom,
I reach for the stars through you.
Always have, always will. I love you.
—M

Acknowledgments

To my husband — Brandon, thank you for supporting me on this journey. You never doubted this publishing dream of mine, even when I did. You always told me my work was good enough, and I couldn't give up. There's nothing I want more in this world than to make you and our boys proud. You've loved me for so long it's a part of who I am and who I'll always be. There's nothing like what we have, and there's not supposed to be. It's ours, and I love living this love song with you. I love you— forever.

To my editor — Kylee Howells, thank you for all the time and effort you put into AB. I can't tell you how much I appreciate you for being a champion of my work and for believing in it. I hope to work with you again.

To my publisher — Literary Wanderlust, LLC, thank you for believing in a new author and seeing the promise in my work. To the entire team at LW, thank you for the roles you played in getting this novel published. I am very grateful.

1

Stupid Boy

Forrest Locke stepped off the plane at O'Hare International Airport and headed straight for the terminal bar. What the hell was he thinking, coming to Chicago to confront his ex-wife and her new lover—his brother?

He slid onto a barstool, confirmation for his flight back home to Fairbanks, Alaska already in his hand. He was a man of the law, and legally, he had no recourse against Jessica and Sam. Even if they'd been having an affair long before he'd known about it, beating the shit out of his brother wasn't going to fix anything.

At least he didn't have to go back through airport security.

"What can I get you?" The bartender made a heavy-handed pour into a ball glass.

Forrest caught the NFL scores running across the bottom of the flat screen above the bar. "Damn Panthers," he muttered. Even his team couldn't catch him a break. "I need a beer. Can I get a Goose Island?"

"Sure, man. One second."

Swarms of people passed by as he settled in to wait for his flight back home. Some filtered inside, filling the bar to capacity except for the last seat beside him. He watched as a young woman in black heels, a hip-hugging charcoal skirt, and a white blouse raced around the other airport dwellers. Her fuchsia wool coat bounced in her arms as she pulled her carry-on, and his heart pounded as she neared. Too pretty. Too-too pretty.

She dropped her belongings behind the empty stool and rested tan fingers on the back of the chair. "Is someone sitting here?"

Sea blue eyes locked with his, and he devolved into a caveman, grunting and shaking his head in response. She was like the northern lights—stunning enough to rob a man of his words and bright enough to light up the sky.

Breathe.

Pink nails skimmed over her pinned back blonde hair. "Thank God."

She lifted her leg to get on the stool, but the fabric of her skirt caught, and she froze on one foot. Forrest muffled a laugh as she hopped her ass up onto the seat. It earned him an icy stare from Blue Eyes, and he washed it down with a swig of cold beer. Practicality and women never seemed to go together.

Gazes swung their way, gravitating toward her like lost planets searching for a womanly sun. Some of them were subtle, others brazen in a way she masterfully ignored. He wouldn't be vying for this celestial trophy tonight, though. At thirty-nine, he was too old, and wouldn't have stood a chance in his younger days, either.

"Got some I.D., sweetheart?" The bartender shoved a towel in his back pocket. It fell as he smiled at her.

She thumbed it out of her wallet and slapped it on the bar top.

The bartender read it and his eyes narrowed. *Fake I.D.?* No one needed a drink bad enough to throw false identification around a government-regulated building crawling with law enforcement officers. Not even Forrest.

The bartender held the shiny, square piece of plastic up, comparing it to her face. "Date of birth?"

She recited it with just the slightest, angry twang.

"All right." He handed the I.D. back. "First one's on me."

Twenty-four? Forrest gave her the once over again. She looked fresh out of college, small but somehow intimidating beside his six-feet-three, two hundred and twenty pounds.

"Can I get..." She paused, gaze darting to the flat screen. "Damn Panthers. Can I get a Miller Lite? Bottle, please."

Forrest glanced between her and the highlights reel. "You too, huh?"

She crossed her legs in his direction, and he had to right himself, staring at her tanned, toned calves.

"I'm from North Carolina." Her southern accent caressed the words right out of her mouth. "What's your excuse?"

Forrest had always rooted for the Seahawks as a kid because of his old man. Football was the only reason they'd ever talked about loyalty and heart. When their relationship fell apart, so did Forrest's love for the team.

Half a beer down, and he was already thinking about his childhood. It was going to be a rough night.

"Alaska doesn't have a team," he said.

The shadow of a smile on her face vanished, and she tucked an invisible stray hair behind her ear. "Well, at least we're loyal."

"Doesn't seem to be doing anybody any good, though." He turned away from her, football and real-life blending in a way he couldn't handle.

After Sports Center wrapped up the berating of his team, he peeked back at the young woman, and her eyes were closed. She breathed purposely in and out. It was in his blood to help people, and he didn't know if she needed help, but she needed something.

"It helps if you relax your shoulders," he whispered.

Her bunched-up shoulders fell, and she sucked in a long, steady breath. "Thank you."

Forrest knew how to calm himself down. It was part of his job when not only people were trying to kill him and each other, but animals too. Not to mention the ever-changing weather of Alaska's interior.

But he couldn't ignore the listlessness in her voice. Even though she was a grown woman, he still worried. "Is there a reason you're so far from home?"

She picked at the label on her beer bottle. "I was offered my dream job this morning."

"Shouldn't you be happy about that?" His gut had told him it was no simple case of fear of flying. Getting people to open up, to talk to him, fixed a lot of the situations he came across.

She shrugged and pulled her bottom lip between her

teeth. "I got lucky. I asked for relocation after I found out..."

He turned toward her, desperate to hear someone else's story in order to block out his own.

"I found out my boyfriend is expecting a child. Obviously, not with me." She wrapped her arm around her flat stomach and bit down harder on her quivering lip.

Forrest's own chest heaved.

"I don't understand why I wasn't enough." She balled her hands into fists. "I'm sorry. I shouldn't be saying this."

His pain clawed its way to the surface. "You're too young to think like that," he said. "Believe me. It'll eat away at you."

She wiped a tear before it fell. "Sounds like you know something about that."

Those sad eyes coaxed the words the right out of him. "My divorce was finalized today, and my wife—" He had to stop that. "Ex-wife, couldn't run off with my brother fast enough."

Her focus shifted to his left hand. The ghost of his ring was nearly gone.

"That's horrible," she sniffled.

Forrest worried she wouldn't be the only one crying in a few minutes. For some reason, saying it out loud made it so much more real. The life he knew was gone.

"You know why these things happened to us?" A ragged breath shook her.

Forrest shrugged, a lump forming at the back of his throat.

"It's because we're Panthers' fans." Tears spilled

past her grin.

He laughed for the first time in months. Heads shot up around the bar as he buried his face in his hands, body shaking with hysteria. Smiling didn't even feel right. It was so foreign, but he couldn't stop. A five-day-old beard rubbed against his palms. How rough must he look?

Catching the tail end of an easy, infectious laugh, he lifted his head. The young woman wiped away the wetness on her face and leaned back in her chair, smiling.

"I needed that," he admitted. Some of his sadness drifted away, and he didn't care that it would be back.

She ran her fingers over her scalp and released the bun at the nape of her neck. Golden waves spilled down her back, and all Forrest could think to do was wrap his hands in them. He cradled his beer instead.

"The Panthers are good for something, I guess." She gathered most of her hair and pulled it over one shoulder. "You said Alaska. Is that where you're heading?"

"Yes. Seattle then Fairbanks."

"Seattle, Anchorage, and then the North Slope for me."

Fairbanks was a large city in the interior of Alaska with some of the country's most extreme weather conditions. Anchorage was temperate in comparison. The North Slope was another world all its own. Forrest sighed. Odds weren't great their paths would cross again.

"I'm familiar with most of what the state has to offer," he said. "But what's taking you to the Arctic? Research?"

The family business he'd left ten years ago relied heavily on environmental research to manipulate the fishing industry. Corruption and a never-ending power struggle with his father had set him on a new course in life, and now he wouldn't trade it for anything.

Just as she opened her mouth to speak, the bartender placed a shot of clear liquid in front of her. "From the guy over there."

Across the bar, a group of young men watched Forrest and his new friend. They were well-dressed and clean-shaven. The one with a red scarf hanging around his neck raised his shot glass.

She sat back, eyeing the tiny glass as if it might've been tainted. "Can't they see I'm with someone?"

Forrest's ego almost knocked down the man sitting next to him. Even if she was using him to ward off unwanted attention, he'd take it. The day hadn't gone to hell after all.

"They thought he might be," the bartender grimaced, "family?"

She didn't even resemble him with her light hair, heart-shaped face, and sun-kissed skin. Green-eyed with dark brown hair, he had fair skin and a square jaw. Old Wranglers, boots, and a plaid flannel shirt under his coat should have made it easy for anyone to see they were worlds apart.

Forrest locked eyes on the jackass with the scarf. Even out of uniform, he managed to get the young man to look away.

"He's not my father." She scooted the shot glass toward the bartender.

It was hell after all. If there had been a hole near him, Forrest would have fallen in head first. Maybe he could dig one beneath his barstool.

"We need a couple more beers," she said.

Forrest froze as she turned into him, knees resting between his widespread legs.

Ever since news of his separation broke, women seemed more drawn to Forrest than usual. He didn't know if it was the rumors of his family's wealth, his badge, or his looks. In the last year, he'd packed on twenty pounds of muscle passing time in the gym. He was in the best shape of his life, but it didn't change the fact he was childless and wifeless at an age when most thought he shouldn't be. What did this girl see in him?

She rested her head in her hand. "I should have given you that shot."

He had to get his shit together. "Probably could have used it."

Blouse gaping, she leaned forward to brush something off her leg, making her breasts spill over the cups of her zebra-striped bra. The panties had to match. A woman didn't walk out of the house all put together and forget that small detail. Even if they didn't, he'd die to find out, and he'd be a happy dead man.

The blood coursing through his body warmed him all over. He shoved his sleeves up his forearms. "I'm Forrest, by the way."

"I'm Patience." She smiled, taking his outstretched hand.

The moment his hand touched hers, his breath hitched. And damn it. He blushed.

人

Patience Cline loved the feel of Forrest's calloused hand. He was built for the dangers of the last frontier with thick arms and legs and amazingly broad shoulders.

Chris—her ex-boyfriend—was an average-sized man with biweekly trimmed hair, a wardrobe larger than hers, and a runner's body. Right now, she struggled to miss him. Someone so different sat beside her, and they happened to be paddling in the same holey canoe.

When she'd ordered two shots of tequila to go with their beers, Forrest hadn't protested. Now they each had a sprinkle of salt and a slice of lime in their hands. He took in a deep breath.

"I'll make sure you get on the plane," she promised.

"I'll be fine." He raised the glass short of his lips.

"Next round, we'll get the kind with the pretty gold flecks in it," she teased.

"Hilarious." He clanked his glass with hers. "Cheers."

Just the hint of a smile on his lips pushed her worries away. Erasing, or at least blurring some of his troubles made her feel good. The deal she'd gotten wasn't as raw as his, but it was enough to push her to tears every second she thought about it. Chris had said he loved her. Claimed he still did, but it was impossible to know. Especially since she had no idea what love was.

Based on Forrest's appearance alone, she couldn't begin to fathom what kind of woman would turn away from this rugged, quiet man. Even his forearms were turning her insides into mush. He was a little older than her, but so what? There was plenty of worse company to have on a layover.

She licked the salt from her hand, threw back the shot, and sucked on the lime, using the juice to wash the familiar burn down. Yum.

Forrest slammed the shot glass down and snatched his beer up, chasing the liquor.

Lightweight.

"You know..." He held his hand to his chest. "That old boyfriend of yours, he's a stupid boy."

Chuckles kept the tears from falling down Patience's face. She hadn't known Chris. Plain and simple.

"You're right," she admitted. "And your brother sounds like a real dick."

How could family do that to each other? Who ran off with their brother's ex-wife? Patience adored her brother, a marine serving overseas in God-knows-where. Their father hadn't been the parent they needed after their mother had died, but the men in her life would never hurt her, or each other. Not intentionally.

The smile dissipated from Forrest's green eyes. "Let's get another shot."

"If you can handle it." She didn't mean to emasculate him, but he'd choked down the last one. Patience wasn't exactly proud of her college days, but she couldn't deny they weren't far behind her either.

"Two more shots," he called to the bartender.

If he wanted to play, she could hang all night long.

Never taking his stare away from her, he shrugged off his coat and undid the top two buttons of his red and white plaid shirt. Patience's hands itched to latch onto his sleeve-stretching biceps.

Her phone vibrated, then started ringing her and Chris's song. Pretty lyrics—now pretty lies. Forrest asked, "Is that him?"

She nodded, wishing the device would shatter into a million pieces. All she wanted was a few minutes where her mind wasn't wandering back to him.

"Can I answer?"

She handed the device over. Goodbye old life.

"Hello?" he answered, his tone deeper than a moment ago.

She could barely make out Chris's voice. She'd be unreachable during her month training at sea, and it couldn't happen soon enough. The embarrassment of being the other woman was hacking away at her dignity.

"This is Alaska State Trooper Forrest Locke. Who's this?" he demanded.

Trooper? Patience's mind undressed then redressed him in a police uniform. A uniform equipped with handcuffs. A sexy cop to nurse her breakup? Jackpot.

"She doesn't want to speak to you...It's none of your business." More silence from Forrest and then, "Hold on. I'll show you."

Instinctively, she leaned into him as he leaned into her. Before the camera flashed, she planted a kiss on his cheek and didn't realize she had been gripping his thigh until it tensed. She pulled away from his short whiskers, trying to restore their personal space, worried she'd crossed a line, but he tugged her barstool toward him. In one easy motion, their chairs were touching.

"Here it comes, Chris." Forrest turned the speakerphone on.

"Patience, are you even there?"

She cringed. How had her life turned upside down so quickly?

"Yeah, baby," she drawled. "I'm here." *Here without you.*

"Come home, sweetheart. I want to talk. Are you in trouble?" There was nothing left to talk about. He was a salesman, and she had taken the bait like she was starving.

"I'm not coming back. I'm moving to Alaska." There. She said it.

"*What*?" he gasped, followed by silence. Patience stilled, and Forrest patted her hand. Chris had gotten the picture. "That's a real nice lumberjack you got there, Pay." A damn hot lumberjack. "Hey, buddy, she likes it from the back like a bitch. Give it to her real hard for me."

"You—" Forrest yelled as she jerked the phone away.

"When he does," she said, as sinister as she could, "I'll be screaming his name."

Patience's face burned, and the throbbing between her ears pounded out of control.

The part of the bar in earshot erupted in applause, and for a second her shame was easier to carry. She could fuck whoever she wanted. Chris had been doing it all along when she had been faithful. She had the habit of putting her heart into everything she did. It was a habit she needed to break.

Forrest's eyes were wide as he took in the scene. At least he got to see her side of the story.

By the time the clapping hands in the bar went silent, so did Chris. Their connection was over. Over for good.

The bartender placed two more shots on the bar. "On the house," he whispered.

Forrest hesitated at first but nudged his glass next to hers in quiet cheers. She did the same and let the lava down her throat take her away. When she came back, all she could do was stare at the glassy-eyed man next to her. He'd kick Chris's ass.

"That was a lot nicer than what I would have said,"

he mumbled. "I definitely wouldn't have made it on the plane."

Patience didn't know if it was the alcohol or him making her feel funny inside. "Really?"

"Really," he confirmed. "Men shouldn't talk about women that way."

She stared at her hands in her lap. "Probably something I should have picked up on a long time ago."

There had been plenty of signs she and Chris were headed for Doomsville, but they didn't become obvious until the aftermath. Maybe if she hadn't studied so much, maybe if she hadn't taken an internship every summer, their two years together wouldn't be merely a bad memory now.

Forrest lifted her chin. The hard seriousness of his face probably scared criminals shitless on the daily, but she could see through it. See the pain hiding in his emerald eyes.

"You're just one person closer to the one you're supposed to be with." His Adam's apple rolled. "Okay?"

She exhaled, hoping the release would somehow keep the tears from spilling down her cheeks. "Okay, Trooper Locke."

He smiled softly and dropped his hand. "Tell me, Patience. Why in the hell are you going to Alaska?"

Her blossoming career, her passion, was plenty to be happy about. "I'm a marine mammal observer. I speak for the whales."

He laughed, and she punched his arm. Researching endangered whale species was her dream. They couldn't speak for themselves, so she would do it for them. Protect them. Someone had to.

"It's not funny." She fought to keep a straight face.

"You're right, it's not." He took two long gulps of his beer, smiling around the bottle's rim. "MMOs are important to the state's marine life. I can drink to that."

The time of her life was ahead of her. "I've got some training to do in Anchorage, and then I'll be in Deadhorse for all of October."

His brow rose. "Aside from the oil fields, it's a beautiful place. And dangerous."

"I know." She twirled a lock of hair tightly around her finger.

The subzero temperatures weren't the only intimidating factors in Deadhorse. Researchers hadn't been exactly welcomed this year. The results of their aerial survey would determine if whale populations were stable enough for offshore drilling in the Beaufort Sea. Patience couldn't worry about the oil community right now—she had a job to do.

"Fairbanks is the closest trooper outpost to Deadhorse." Forrest smiled. "If you need anything, it might take us a couple of days, but we'll get there. North Slope Borough PD's not far either, depending on the weather."

She shrugged. "Well, if you need a pen pal in the Arctic to talk Panther football with, I might know someone."

Did I just hit on him? She flagged the bartender for another round.

"Yeah?" He asked. A curious glint filled his eyes as he leaned back.

She took him in as he did her, the pink tint in his cheeks warming her from the inside out. "Yeah."

Time lost itself in their laughter. Patience kept the floor open for Forrest to speak, encouraging his unpracticed jokes and soaking up his little bits of wisdom. He'd lived a lot more than she had, but it didn't leave her feeling like she was lacking. It gave her the sense everything would be okay.

Forrest slumped back in his seat, staring at the list of departures on the screen above the bar. He called for the bartender and jumped clumsily to his feet.

"Flight's canceled." Like a doll, he lifted her off the barstool and put her on her feet. "We have to hurry to make sure we get on the next flight."

Patience dug in her purse for money. Forrest's badge flashed beneath his shirt as he threw a hundred behind the bar. Both of their carry-ons rolled behind him as he headed to their airline's booth.

Forrest claimed they were lucky to get on the connecting flight to Seattle tomorrow afternoon. Patience had to get a hotel and dedicate a whole extra day to flying now. As if he had gone through this before, Forrest called local hotels over and over while she struggled to find numbers. All of the travelers around them were on the phone. What the hell was going on? She listened closely. Lightening? Control tower?

"Thank you," Forrest sighed into the phone then touched the end button. "The Hilton attached to the airport is booked, but they got me a room at another one of their hotels. The Wit is about ten miles away."

Patience shoved the panic rising in her throat down. She rarely traveled. Had never done so unaccompanied by family. The last thing she wanted to do was call her father. She was on her own now and had to fix her own problems. Her funds were limited because, as she had explicitly told her father, she could take care of herself. Her employer would reimburse her expenses, but she was nearing her last dollar.

Nausea rolled with the list of area hotels in her phone. What was she doing here? How much did hotel rooms cost? And cabs? The further away the more expensive.

She could call her team leader in Anchorage, but it was late, and she was hell-bent on making a good impression.

She closed the webpage and found her father's name in her contacts.

"There's also a canceled music festival adding to the mess here." Forrest waved his hand around.

Someone claimed a bench and stretched out on top of it. She could drink until tomorrow afternoon, but what if there wasn't a man to buy her drinks?

Really?

She dropped her phone and caught it off her knee. How had drinks with a sexy trooper taken such a turn for the worse? Being lost in him was so much better than the real world.

"You've had a lot to drink." Forrest looked around then checked his watch. "I can't leave you to fend for yourself out here."

"I'll figure something out." She rubbed her head, ready to call her father. *He's never going to let you leave home again.* "I had a really good time tonight, Forrest. Really, I did."

He shook his head. "I got a suite. It's all they had. Come with me."

Patience locked eyes with him, unsure who was

tipsier. "Are you sure?"

"Of course." He held his hand out for her carry-on.

She slid the handle into his palm and hooked her arm inside his. "Maybe we can talk some more?"

A wave of pink swept across his face, and he smiled. "I'd love that, Patience."

They hurried out into the crisp night air, the butterflies in her stomach carrying her over the rain-speckled ground as thunder rolled and lightning flashed around them.

2

Black

Forrest followed Patience inside the suite, inhaling wildflowers. If he closed his eyes, he'd be in the meadow behind his house during the springtime. How could she smell like home?

City lights speckled the floor-to-ceiling windows, fighting the glare of two end table lamps. Pops of color softened the hard lines of the modern suite in the red sofa pillows and the blue and green marble-filled vases on the kitchen counter.

He placed her carry-on in the bedroom beside the king-sized bed she'd have all to herself. Man, he hoped the living room sofa was a pull-out.

He only got close enough to the floor-to-ceiling window to see the tip of the burnt-orange Chicago theatre sign in the living area as Patience stared down at the city. A chirping came from her coat pocket, and she removed her phone, shaking her head at the screen.

"Everything all right?" he asked.

She shrugged, pulling her bottom lip between her teeth again. "You don't want to know what he's saying."

He didn't need it verbatim. Her defeated tone was enough.

"When you get to Alaska..." He shoved his hands in his pockets, unsure if she would want his help. "If he's still bothering you, there are steps you can take to make it stop. I can help you file a report."

She smiled, dropping the phone to her side. "I bet you look great in uniform."

He'd bet she'd look great in anything. Nothing. He couldn't think about that. She was in a bad place and just because he was too didn't mean he could want her the way he did.

"We should probably check the weather." He snatched the remote control off the coffee table and pressed the power button.

Quiet jazz music played in the background of the next day's forecast, and it did nothing to calm his nerves. The highs and lows and the chance of precipitation weren't enough to distract him from Patience taking off her coat, and strolling over to him.

"Are you really worried about the weather?" she asked.

No. I don't give a shit about the weather.

"Just wondering if we'll get delayed tomorrow." If he breathed any deeper, he might touch her, but he wouldn't dare move.

She took the remote from his suddenly weak hand and turned off the television. "Tell me about your job, Trooper Locke."

He could listen to her say "Trooper Locke" all night long.

"Um..." His stomach muscles clenched as she lifted his shirt to expose his badge. "I..."

"Go on. I'm listening."

"Keep the peace." He closed his eyes, the warmth of her palms on his sides traveling to places she hadn't even reached yet. "Enforce the law, prevent and detect crime, protect—"

"It sounds like you're reading from a textbook."

That's how he liked it. He was a professional. Careful. Always had been.

"Do you arrest a lot of people?" She tilted her head to the side.

He nodded, an image of her handcuffed and bent over the hood of his patrol car blazing through his mind.

"How do you frisk someone?"

Fingers teased his waistband. She didn't want him to frisk her, did she? His face burned.

"You'd have them put their hands on the back of their head," He swallowed as she raised his arms. He interlaced his fingers at the back of his head. This couldn't be happening. "Then you'd have them spread their legs."

She glanced at his boots, and his feet spread apart. How did she have him at her mercy so fast?

"Then I do this?" She pressed her body against his and ran her hands along his forearms and down his biceps. He flexed involuntarily.

"Not quite." His cock stirred, and he pulled his hips back.

"Are you sure?" She smoothed his loose shirt down

his sides.

It didn't matter where he looked. Her eyes. Her hands. Her breasts. The ceiling. He couldn't tamper his arousal enough to stop her.

He wanted it. Whatever she tempted him with, he would gladly try, even if it was just a taste.

"Your hands—" He hissed as she took his phone out of his front pocket, grazing the edge of his growing flesh. "You're supposed to use the back of your hands."

She tossed his phone on the couch. Then his wallet. "I don't like that."

It was the law when searching a person of the opposite sex, but how could he tell her when she palmed him with both hands, feeding his erection with a wonderful pressure.

"You have the right to remain silent." The corner of her mouth pulled up, and the end of his belt slid through the buckle.

"Am I under—" He groaned as his cock sprung free of his pants and she held him, never taking her gaze away from his face.

"Oh, you're under arrest, Trooper Locke."

She stroked him, melting away the stupid grin on his face. It felt too good. Borderline tease. Borderline enough. If he could just get his hands on her.

Sweat coated his brow and the back of his neck, fighting the cool air pouring down from the ceiling. She gripped him tighter, moved her hand more purposefully.

Keep it together, Forrest.

With one hand, she worked down the buttons of her blouse. Black and white lace cupped her breasts. Voluptuous for her petite frame, but perfect for his hands.

He sighed.

Once she was naked, he'd be a goner. There'd be no turning back. A long-ignored hunger tried to win him over now, even though he knew she was hurting, and it was pain that sent her into his arms in the first place.

He fought every instinct, nearly failed to block out the pleasurable coaxing of her hand. "Patience, I don't know if I can."

I don't know if I should.

She let him go and he bit his tongue at the loss. The blouse fell over her shoulders as she stepped back and unzipped her skirt. It slid down her tan legs like a silk sheet.

His heart hammered. He just wanted his world to go black, black like the lace bands flaring around the curves of her hips. A tiny triangle of white hid the junction between her thighs.

Jesus Christ.

He spun around and tucked himself back in his jeans.

Relax. You need this.

He fumbled down the buttons of his shirt, heat trapped between his skin and his clothes feeding a fire he needed to slow.

Cool fingers skimmed beneath the flannel.

"Forrest." She leaned against his back. "I don't want to be his anymore."

All the nerves radiating through his chest morphed into a dull ache. He didn't want to belong to Jessica anymore either. For the past year, he'd been trying to turn it off like it was some kind of faulty switch.

It was selfish and reckless, but Patience could be his

tonight.

He turned around and took her face in his hands, all his fears lost in the blue of her eyes. She kissed him before he could take a breath. The mix of tequila and the taste of someone new blended in the swirl of her tongue until his cock pulsed against his jeans. He inhaled her. Delved into her open mouth.

With a fistful of his shirt, she tugged him closer, but it would never be close enough for him.

He pulled away, hoping she was still willing to play. "Let me show you how to do it right."

"Excuse me?" She panted, a frown scrunching up her beautiful face. "Was I doing something wrong?"

He chuckled and ushered her back to the window. "Hands on the glass, Miss."

She whipped around to the night lights and smacked her hands against the window.

"First, you need probable cause to search someone." He caught her ass before she could rub it against him.

So impatient.

"If you're going to search someone," He ran his hands over her round, bare cheeks. "You always do it from behind."

人

Patience's breaths fogged the window. Moments ago she'd been trying to coax Forrest out of his pants, and now he had her on display for State Street.

"Why from behind?" she asked.

"I'm less vulnerable at someone's back."

Careful hands came over her shoulders, sliding up her arms and resting on top of her hands. Heat blanketed her back while the chilly night snuck through the glass at her front. She closed her eyes, feeling anything but vulnerable inside his strong arms. Happy to pretend this wasn't a one-night stand and the world wasn't going to rear its ugly face in the morning.

The warmth of his embrace faded as his arms fell away. It rekindled in her core as his hot mouth dragged along the tendon in her neck. He slipped the lace cups of her bra aside, letting her breasts spill into his hands.

"Is this how you search all your suspects, Trooper Locke?"

He pinched her nipples with just enough pressure to send a jolt straight to her pussy. She bit her lip to keep from moaning, struggled to hold it in when a hand drifted down her back and fingers followed the lace between her ass cheeks.

"No." He kissed her shoulder. "I haven't met someone quite like you."

Even if it was just pretend, emotion lodged in her throat that he might actually see her differently.

A finger slid inside her from behind, and she exhaled a massive breath. His other hand reached down the front of her, spreading her lips and rubbing her wetness against her clit. Another digit entered her, and her knees buckled.

"Forrest..." She rested her forearms against the window, unable to catch her breath between his wall-stretching thrusts and the teasing passes over her swollen bud of nerves.

His mouth was hot against her ear. "I bet you taste wonderful."

Desperation scorched up her neck and face. "Then

taste me."

She turned around at the loss of his touch, catching herself against the cool glass. Layers of muscle stared back at her as he dropped his shirt onto the floor. She didn't get a chance to admire him before he fell to his knees.

She squealed as he tossed one of her legs over his shoulder and then the other. The window held her upright. Keeping one hand plastered against its flat surface, she threaded the other through his dark hair.

Seducing him had been wrong in so many ways, but none of them seemed wrong enough as his tongue traveled leisurely from her entrance to her clit. She pressed against the glass, ignoring his whiskers scratching the insides of her thighs.

Tingles branched out from her spine as he sucked and nibbled on her labia. She jerked when he flicked his tongue across her pulsing clit, grabbing as much of his short hair as she could to keep from falling off his shoulders. He held her up, hands under her ribcage, pinning her to the window. Safe under his control, she calmed and lost herself in the slow, firm circles going over her sensitive bud. Eyes closed, trusting the rhythm of his tongue, she let the wave build from her toes. Her own whimpers floated up to her ears as his hands climbed to her breasts and worked her nipples.

"Oh, God." She gnashed her teeth, trying to back away from the precipice. "Forrest...wait."

He slowed to a near stall.

"Too slow." She squirmed. "Too slow."

He sucked her clit into his hot mouth and her orgasm blossomed violently through her arms and legs. She thrashed under his restraint, bucking into his mouth with each pulse of ecstasy racking up her body.

Afraid she would explode from the intensity, she scrambled to get down. He caught her in his lap, his chest heaving and eyes wild. She had no idea a stranger could make her feel this way.

He kissed her, bringing her to her feet and spreading her essence through her mouth as he carried her to the dining room table. Papers rustled and a chair thumped against the floor. Something skidded across the tabletop until it cracked against the ground.

He lay her down, bracing himself above her. "Tell me you have a condom."

"Purse." She pointed around the suite, unsure where she'd left the damn thing and praying a condom would surface in the oversized handbag.

Forrest found it and shook out its contents all over the floor. She flipped over on the table, and he paused, eyes locked on her ass in the air.

"Hurry," she pled over her shoulder.

He picked through her things then jumped to his feet, ripping the little plastic square open with his teeth.

The cool tabletop pressed against her face as a hot length slid across her pussy. A ball of anticipation knotted in her stomach.

The head nudged her entrance, and she sighed, eager to get the entirety of him seated inside her. When he pushed again, harder this time, she bit her lip and surged back. The air slipped from her lungs.

"Fuck, Patience." He stilled, fingers digging into her hips.

She stretched around him, breaths coming easier as

she accommodated his girth.

Inch by inch, he withdrew from her body then sank all the way back in. He murmured up her back and down her arms to where her hands gripped the table's edge. He moved inside her maddeningly slow. Over and over. Every nerve in her body hummed, thirsting for another release. She rocked back against him uncontrollably, need and frustration twisting together.

"*Forrest*," she begged.

Finally, he slammed into her, obliterating his leisurely pace. She couldn't hear her moans over their bodies knocking against the table but could feel them vibrating in her throat like the little spasms erupting inside her channel.

Forrest reared her back by her hair and kissed her so deeply her eyes flew open. Her orgasm came in electric waves to the sound of his shouts, and she rode them until the last ripple, buried beneath his body.

He skimmed his lips across her shoulders. Wisps of kisses tingled her skin between heavy breaths, and her heart soaked the affection up before she could even warn it not to. What had this man done to her? She wouldn't dare stop him from nuzzling her neck like a lover, refusing to believe their afterglow would fade into the night.

3

Fly

Forrest ran his fingers through Patience's hair. Even in the overcast morning light, she shined, head on his chest and arm strewed across his waist. He and Jessica had never slept this way, always back to back no matter how good or bad their day had been.

It was strange to share a bed with someone new. He couldn't shake the fear of not doing it again with Patience. He'd only invested one night in her, but it was one night more than anybody else since the divorce.

Starting his life over would be hard, but he wasn't used to things being easy. Before he could start this day, he needed to answer the dozens of texts on his phone.

He pulled his arm out from underneath her and slipped out of the bed, making sure to keep her under the covers. His jeans lay strewn atop his luggage, and he pulled them on up to his hips and went to the next room.

A light fog floated outside the windows, leaving tiny

drops of water on the glass. The contents of Patience's purse were everywhere. Chairs lay on their sides, and the dining room table wobbled as he brushed by it.

He sat in an oversized polka-dot chair at the other end of the suite and called his cousin and fellow trooper, Logan.

"Hey, fuck-face. How's Chicago?"

Forrest rubbed his eyes. "How do you know I'm in Chicago?"

"Between the plane ticket and the five-hundred-dollars-a-night suite?"

"You have got to stop hacking my shit."

"Had you told me you were on the warpath to murder your brother, I could have come with you."

"I didn't murder anyone."

"Tell me you at least beat him to within an inch of his life. Cause when you didn't show up for pool last night, I had to let Dawson be my partner, and I don't think I need to tell you how much ass he sucked."

"Give the rookie a chance." He chuckled. "And no, I came to my senses before the plane landed. I don't know what I was thinking."

"You serious?" he asked.

"Yeah."

"You went all that way for nothing?

"It wouldn't have done me any good." He could never move forward if he stayed in the past.

"Well, you sound better than I expected. I didn't really know what to expect, honestly."

Logan was the little brother Forrest never had. From childhood until the day Logan partied out of college, Forrest had stood by him when their family severed ties and their money, picking him up from rehab, and pushing him into the trooper academy. Now the one who had struggled and fought inner demons every day was checking up on him.

A long time ago, it would have been Sam checking on Forrest, but that ship had sunk.

"I'm all right," he said. "Thanks."

"We'll get you moved out and into the cabin when you get back, okay?"

"Sounds good."

The bedroom door opened. Patience mouthed the word "Sorry" and tip-toed away, hands failing to cover her breasts and butt. He grinned.

"I have to go," he said. "I'll check in when I get back."

Patience let the steam out of the bathroom door, keeping the towel around her tight enough to subdue the butterflies in her stomach. Forrest sat on the end of the bed, his gaze drifting up to meet hers. It was like seeing him for the first time all over again.

A man in desperate need of a shave and a haircut—with the scars of his job hidden in the contours of his body, and the scars of a failed marriage hidden in his eyes—shouldn't stun her the way he did. Shouldn't make her want to hold him until he *saw* her in his dreams and not that bitch he mumbled about in his sleep.

He stood, but her damn legs wouldn't walk her out of the bathroom. She had to get by without touching him or there would be no time for breakfast. Warmth seeped into her skin as he walked into the bathroom and she stumbled out.

He turned around and gripped the top of the doorframe, arms bowing around his head. "Hungry?"

The thin expanse of dark hair across his chest led her down to his sculpted abs, then to the V of his hips and undone jeans.

I'll just have you for breakfast.

She swallowed. "Room service?"

"Menu's in the kitchen." He licked his lips then shut the door.

Patience didn't bother dressing.

Before browsing through the room service menu, she dropped to the floor beside her purse and gathered her things. As she scooped up lipstick, an earring, and loose change off the couch, she caught a heavy ring. *Maybe the previous occupants had left it behind?* Engraved on the inside of the ring were two sets of initials and date: *FAL & JML 2004.* Forrest's brown leather wallet lay open on the couch where she'd tossed it last night.

She dropped the wedding band and wrung out the end of her towel until her hands turned red.

Don't freak out.

Pressure built in her chest until she choked out a sob. If he was divorced, why would he still have his wedding band? She thought back to the bar. Had he been wearing it when she'd sat down? It wouldn't have been the first time a married man had tried to pick her up.

How could she let this happen? It explained why he'd been so nervous the night before. It hadn't been timidity—just guilt.

His poor wife. She scratched at her arms, unable to keep her skin from crawling.

Somehow everything that had fit in her purse the

night before didn't want to fit now. She grabbed what she could and dumped the towel on the sofa. Blouse half-buttoned and skirt unzipped, she jumped in her heels and found her coat.

The water was still running when she snuck her carry-on out of the bedroom door.

She couldn't be the *other* woman. Not twice. Not ever again. She wouldn't be lured to breakfast one more time just to have her heart broken over eggs benedict. Chris had told her to meet him at their favorite cafe, only to ruin the place by telling her about six-month pregnant Bethany.

Tears came harder than they did yesterday. Somehow, she managed to find the lobby button in the elevator. What was she thinking about, moving across the country? It didn't matter where she was, she'd always make mistakes.

She managed to get her damp hair into a bun by the time the elevator doors opened. Fingers rushing down the buttons of her coat, she hurried through the lobby and ran outside into the cold, busy street to hail a cab. There was just enough money in her purse to pay the driver when she reached the airport.

On a bench outside the Delta Airlines booth, she dabbed her face with her sleeves, ignoring passersby. She took out her phone, scrolled through her contacts and pressed the call button. Her father had been right. Running from her problems wouldn't fix them.

"Cline and Watson Finance and Accounting," answered her father's assistant. "This is Brenda. How can I help you?"

"Brenda, it's Patience."

"Oh, sweetheart. Your father told me everything. He's trying to get Chris disbarred. Let me grab him. He's about to go deep-sea fishing with a client."

"Brenda," Patience bit out. "I called to talk to *you*."

Hearing the disappointment in her father's voice had always upset Patience more than seeing it on his face. She couldn't speak to him, not after telling him where to stick his money. She wasn't an account he could manage any more.

"Sweetie," Brenda whispered. "What's wrong?"

Everything.

Patience couldn't force the knot at the back of her throat to loosen.

"It's your mom, isn't it?" Brenda asked.

When Patience's mother had passed away, Brenda had been the one to pick her up from softball practice and cello lessons. She even played parent when Patience had gotten kicked out of her dorm for streaking across the quad.

From her perfect bangs to her pink manicures and dress suits, Brenda had been never-changing in Patience's life.

"I think," Patience sniffled, "Mom would be really disappointed in me."

Brenda sighed. "That's not possible, Pay."

If you only knew.

"Did you bring your candle?" Brenda asked.

Patience's mother, Evelyn, had made soy candles in their kitchen every summer to sell at the local farmer's markets. She'd left hundreds behind, and every year Patience would take one to her grandmother's home on Oak Island and light it on the beach.

"Yeah." She took a deep breath. "I have it." The anniversary of her death was coming up soon, and it would be the first year she talked to her mother from someplace other than their special spot.

"I imagine the beach looks a lot different in Alaska," Brenda said.

Air came in spurts through Patience's lungs. "More rocks, fewer Speedos."

"I love a gorgeous landscape as much as the next person," Brenda said, "but a confident, hairy man walking out of the ocean in all his glory is heaven to me, sweetheart."

Patience laughed and wiped her cheeks dry.

Just breathe.

"I'm glad I called."

Brenda's laughter faded. "You're going to be all right, Pay. It'll get easier every day."

"Day one was pretty hard." She pulled her coat button back through the loop.

"Yesterday won't keep you from tomorrow."

Patience huffed. "It might when you're in yesterday's wrinkled clothes that reek of tequila."

"Patience," her father's tone cut through the phone.

She looked around for a man hundreds of miles away even though Alex Cline had picked up the line in his office. He probably had on his favorite faded blue visor and a white polo.

"Hey, Dad."

"Have fun bar hopping in Chicago after your canceled flight last night?" A pen clicked incessantly in the background.

Don't take the bait.

"No, but I did get a room at theWit on State Street with a strange man." She sat up straight and crossed her arms.

She couldn't help herself. Vague versions of the truth had always sent her father over the edge.

"There are no charges on any of your cards from theWit." A door or a desk drawer slammed shut across the country. "He must have been a gentleman."

"You would have liked him. Late thirties, early forties. Married. A Panthers fan too."

"I swear to God, Pay..."

Their last conversation hadn't gone any better. He'd tried talking her out of leaving and had reminded her how stupid she'd been to major in marine science, how blind she'd been about Chris, and how irresponsible and naive she'd been for taking an assignment in Alaska to get away from an ex.

"Why can't you just tell me the truth?" he asked, voice leveling out. "How hard is it for you to tell me if you're all right or not?"

She sighed. "It's got a lot to do with the way you ask, Dad."

Instead of helping her when she needed it, her father had always gone behind her with a broom and swept up her problems. The only direction for her was the one he saw, and no matter how hard she tried to follow it, she always derailed.

"How are you?" he whispered.

She rubbed her chest, the ache too deep to reach. "Same old Pay, Dad. Same old Pay."

人

Forrest took one last look at the suite.

Why'd you leave, Patience?

He'd thrown away a couple of receipts he found on the floor and knew it wasn't the trooper in him that had searched the little pieces of paper for the last name. Finding it did no good. She didn't want him.

Would she even be on the plane? Could he fly for four hours and ignore her? Touch down in Seattle and not even tell her goodbye?

At the airport, he searched for her at the bar and their gate. He tried not to worry, told himself he had no business asking the airline if she'd checked in. He couldn't spend the rest of his life wondering where she'd gone so he hopped on the train to the next terminal and found the gate waiting for a North Carolina bound flight.

Nothing.

Forrest didn't blame her for bailing on him. He had no regrets, but maybe she did. If he could only tell her to call him if she ever needed help.

The plane was nearly boarded when a flash of fuchsia entered the center aisle. Forrest jumped to his feet. She passed a few empty seats, gaze falling everywhere but where he stood at the back of the plane. When there was only one open seat left for her to take, he met her at that row.

"I was worried about you." He opened the overhead compartment.

She kept her coat on her arm and her bag on the floor. "I got it. Thank you."

He glanced around. Was there some one-night stand etiquette he didn't know about?

"Everything okay?" he asked.

She picked up her carry-on and bumped him in the chest with it, forcing him back a few steps. "Are you really divorced?"

Every head in the surrounding seats lifted.

Forrest straightened his jacket then reorganized the bags in the compartment. "Yes. I told you I was."

She shoved the small suitcase into the space, lips pressed into a straight line as she balled her coat up.

Every scenario he could fathom made zero sense. Did she think he'd lied? Had he crossed a line when he'd asked her to have breakfast with him? What the fuck was going on?

The alcohol had filtered its way out of his body, but his emotions were still raw and ready to attach to anything that made him feel better than the self-induced misery he'd been living in. He was what was wrong.

"I don't know what I did," he said. "I'm sorry for whatever it was."

Patience caught his left hand. A wavy, sun-streaked ponytail fell over her shoulder against her deep blue sweater. Black, short heeled boots didn't give her the height the heels had the night before. Her bright, smooth skin was flawless and her hand unimaginably soft.

She rubbed her thumb across his ring finger. "Forrest, I found your wedding band."

Jesus Christ.

She was too young for his problems, and he should have never put them on her.

"It was on the couch in the living room. I think it fell out of your wallet," she whispered. "I freaked out."

He pulled his wallet out of his back pocket. The indentation of a ring in the leather was smooth under his finger.

"If you're not married..." Patience stepped toward him but kept her focus on his hand. "Then why do you carry it around?"

He couldn't stop his free hand from tilting her chin up. Her eyes stayed cast to the side, and a tiny part of him broke. It mattered that she believed him.

The long-awaited disconnection of his old life had finally come, and he had no idea how to tell her that.

"I want you to understand." He swallowed. "I wouldn't blame you if you didn't, but I really want you to."

She closed her eyes. After the rise and fall of her shoulders, they opened, and his life would never be the same.

"Let's talk after the flight, and save our goodbyes for Seattle." She let his hand go.

4

Get to You

Patience walked with Forrest to her gate in Seattle. This is where they parted ways. She to Anchorage, and he to Fairbanks.

Why does this feel so gut-wrenchingly awful?

"Forrest...I don't think it matters what the truth is." The four-hour flight had turned her thoughts inside out and upside down.

He grimaced and shook his head. "I want it to matter. I want you to know I didn't take advantage of you or your situation."

The tears surfaced, but she blinked them away. "Nothing changes. I'm still getting on that stupid plane, and you're still going to Fairbanks."

He pulled them out of the traffic of the other travelers and leaned their things against the wall.

"Someone broke your heart," he said, palms resting on her shoulders. "They lied to you, hurt you so bad you took a job across the country. I would never do something like that to you, and I need you to know that."

Desperation deepened the hard lines on his face. Patience ignored it. Buried her instincts. Convinced herself it didn't matter how they parted.

But it did.

"I believe you." She didn't care he wasn't over his ex-wife. He couldn't help that. The same way she couldn't help running from every hurdle that jumped in front of her life.

"I've been having a tough time letting go." He brushed a loose lock of hair behind her ear. "I never meant to upset you."

He hadn't meant anything. She was the one who'd liquored him up and seduced him. Patience was in this situation because she'd put herself there.

"I'm sorry, Forrest." She rubbed her forehead. "I'm a mess."

He shrugged, a weak smile lifting his cheeks. "You're a Panther's fan."

The tension in her neck released, and she chuckled. "That I am."

The last call for boarding sounded from her plane's gate, and her pulse went into double time.

Forrest put her coat over her arm and placed the handle to her carry-on in her hand. "You're going to love Anchorage and the North Slope. Maybe after a little while, you can give me a call."

Patience swallowed the knot at the back of her throat. Forward was the only direction she could go. A career waited for her. The whales waited. A new life all her own was just hours away.

The water would be icy, but it was time to jump in.

She stood on her tiptoes and gave Forrest a peck on the lips. "Bye, Trooper Locke."

He crushed her against his chest, and she melted. There was no time for her heart to stretch the way it wanted to.

"I'll talk to you soon," she promised.

He released her slowly, letting go of her hand last. "Bye, Patience."

Four days. It had only been four days, and Patience was second-guessing herself. She leaned her forehead against her locker at the marine mammal institute in Anchorage and shivered. No matter how hot she'd turned the water up, she hadn't been able to shake the cold out of her bones.

A throat cleared behind her, but she didn't have the strength to move.

"It's not as easy as it looks. Is it, princess?"

Patience forced her head to rotate and peered over her shoulder. A woman in a blue and white flight suit examined the ends of her chocolate brown hair. The shiny strands matched her eyes. Undertones of copper warmed her skin. She was stunning.

"That's no way to speak to royalty," Patience muttered, her voice raw from the crisp air.

The woman smirked and tossed her hair aside. "I heard a greenhorn from the east coast finished their survival training today."

Painless breaths just wouldn't come. Patience crumbled against the cold metal. "Doesn't mean I passed."

"From the looks of you—"

Patience glared at the ice queen. "Who are you?"

"I'm Ana," she said. "Pilot for Team October."

October was the final stretch for the annual artic survey. The MMO Patience was replacing had broken both of his legs in a snowmobile accident, and his bad luck could be her good fortune. If she failed survival training, a marine mammal observer from Team September would have to spend an extra month in the Arctic Circle because she wasn't cut out for the job.

A graceful hand spun the knob on her locker door. "What's the combination?"

Patience took a deep breath. Letting strangers down was so much worse than letting her father down. He expected it. They didn't.

Ana sighed. "I don't have all day."

She told Ana the numbers and plopped down on the bench separating the rows of lockers.

"I tried, you know." Patience squeezed the excess moisture out of her hair. "I tried really hard."

Throughout her childhood, she'd gone hunting and fishing with her brother and father. She could survive the outdoors rain or shine, but the cold and the snow of the remote locale she'd been dropped into for two days had infected her muscles and turned them to stone. Hopefully, everything she'd learned wouldn't be locked away in a trauma-induced amnesia file of her brain.

Ana filtered through Patience's clothes, tossing items at her. "Sometimes trying's not enough, and sometimes it is."

Patience forced her arms through her favorite Under

Armour shirt. Could she have tried harder? She should have aced the written part.

Ana pursed her lips, her gaze rising from Patience's numb feet to her tired eyes, and then she smiled. "You passed, princess."

The frigid river Patience had been thrown into to test her survival suit had finally reached her brain. "What did you say?"

Ana threw her hands in the air. "You passed, greenhorn."

Patience collapsed on the bench, arms tangled in her shirt and damp hair strewn across her face. "Damn straight I did."

She could have never faced her father if they had sent her packing.

Ana nudged Patience, nearly knocking her off the bench. "We leave for Deadhorse at six a.m. on Monday."

Patience sighed, pride giving her enough strength to prop herself up. "Deadhorse sounds lovely."

Ana laughed, her teeth pearly white against her deep pink lips. "Hurry up. The guys want to meet you."

Forrest had been back on the job for only a month. Somehow, he was already in his captain's office, hoping Logan's swollen and discolored left hand wasn't the reason for their impromptu meeting.

"How'd that ten-sixteen go?" He glared at his cousin's injured hand. "The one you didn't need backup on?"

Logan tugged on his sleeve. "Textbook."

Domestic disturbance calls had plagued Forrest in his early years as a trooper, but he'd learned to let the justice system hand out the punishment. Logan still struggled from time to time.

"You all right?" Forrest asked.

Logan ran his good hand through his brown hair, the ends of it brushing the tips of his ears. "I'm good. EMS treated the wife at the scene. Her husband got what he deserved."

Forrest didn't need any more explanation. At one point in his life, Logan hadn't cared for anyone but himself. Now he fought for others and put himself on the line every day.

"I guess Dawson or Williams can stand in for you at pool tonight."

Logan's chair skidded back. "Bullshit. I got to win my—"

Captain Thompson walked in belly first and slapped a manila folder down on his desk. He sat and leaned back in his chair, interlacing his fingers at the back of his bald head.

"Your radio work, Trooper Jones?" he asked. "Your phone?"

Logan looked away and nodded.

"Call for backup next time." Captain Thompson ran his hands down his face then planted his elbows on his desk. "Trooper Locke, you and this genius over here..." He cocked his head at Logan. "Are on security detail for the next three weeks."

Forrest shot a warning glance at Logan before a full-blown argument ignited. Logan's chest swelled, but he didn't make a sound.

Captain Thompson handed Forrest the manila folder. "Governor Camden is so impressed with your dedication to the job that he asked for the two of you to join him on his trip to the North Slope."

Forrest and Logan had made the newspapers several times this past summer working on different cases, from rescuing lost hikers on the outskirts of Fairbanks to aiding truckers along the treacherous Dalton Highway to the North Slope. But the Arctic Circle? For three weeks?

Forrest sighed. "The same governor who prides himself on not using a security detail so the troopers can protect the people of Alaska?"

"Same asshole." Captain Thompson pointed to the folder. "His publicist needs to take your pictures for an article."

Logan groaned. "Can't the North Slope Borough Police babysit him?"

Captain Thompson took a sip from his thermos. "It's our job to protect the governor. They're overflowing with oil workers up there, and some of them have had run-ins with a group of researchers. There's a lot of tension."

Forrest thumbed through the file, drifting back to Chicago. "Researchers?"

"Whales, I believe." Captain Thompson swirled his coffee. "I hear another offshore rig is in the works."

Patience smiled, pride filling her eyes. "I'm a marine mammal observer. I speak for the whales."

He laughed, and she punched his arm.

Forrest chuckled.

Logan glared at him. "Camden's only going to make the tension worse."

Governor Camden had signed new leases with Exxon and BP, cutting the oil workers' shares of the profits. Did he really think visiting them and shaking their hands in their extreme work environment would fix what he'd done? He'd even cut the troopers' annual raises, and they were supposed to protect him?

Captain Thompson stood, rubbing his stomach and smacking his lips after a big gulp from his thermos. "Use the next two days to prep for the trip. You'll visit Deadhorse, maybe Barrow. Trooper Jones, get that hand looked at."

Logan stood and flexed his hand, grimacing on his way out. "Sure."

When he disappeared around the corner, Captain Thompson said, "Forrest, after this assignment, we'll talk about that promotion."

Maybe the Arctic wouldn't be so bad. Temperatures would hover around freezing during daylight hours, but it was nothing he couldn't handle. Making Corporal might be just what he needed. A reminder that he was damn good at his job, and no matter the trials in his life, he made a difference in others. There was nothing he guarded more than the law.

$$\bigwedge$$

Forrest placed his bags near the door and took another last look around. Putting his house in the suburbs on the market had been easy. Moving to his summer cabin had been even easier. It took him longer to get to the station and everywhere else he wanted to go, but it was peaceful. He'd always loved it there.

Logan came through the front door. "You got the big screen mounted."

Logan had helped Forrest clean up the place and move the furniture he'd kept. A pool table filled the den, a grill sat on the back porch, and football illuminated the flat screen.

"I should have moved out here sooner." Forrest looked around one more time. "I guess it'll be here when we get back."

"Speaking of our three weeks in frozen hell," Logan said, sitting on the back of the couch. "The Marine Mammal Institute got back to us."

Forrest had hoped for the call. "What'd they have to say?"

"Their teams have resolved whatever troubles they had with the oil field workers while they were still in Deadhorse." Logan shrugged. "Guy asked if we could check in with Team October when we get there, though."

What if Patience was in Deadhorse?

"They're out of Anchorage, right?" Forrest asked. "He say anything about the team members?"

"I think he called from Anchorage." Logan scratched his head. "Didn't say anything about his people, but I'm sure they're a bunch of whacko tree huggers like the rest of them. Why?"

"Curious." Forrest picked up his bags. "I think the governor's been attacked by a conservationist or two... or three."

Logan laughed. "Might be a fun trip after all."

The fun would have to wait. They had a two day ride up the muddy Dalton Highway, and there wouldn't be one mile he'd drive without wondering if Patience was at the end of it.

5

White Lies

Patience pulled her bloody palm away from her mouth. "Ow."

Team October's leader, Paul, sat across from her in the cafeteria at The Aurora Hotel. He crossed his arms and legs. "What happened?"

"I took an elbow to the face." She opened and closed her jaw.

They'd been in Deadhorse, Alaska, a small industrial town within the Arctic Circle, for a week surveying the Beaufort Sea and had already stirred up trouble.

Paul removed his red-framed glasses and rubbed his eyes. White speckles peppered the dark stubble along his chin and the black hair above his ears. Smile lines bowed around his mouth.

"I can see that," he said.

"I was just trying to help."

Joey "Stiller" Wilson held gauze above his eye and

winced in his seat beside Patience. "That asshole sucker punched me."

"I tried to break it up," Patience grumbled. Stupid, stupid, stupid.

"We talked about giving the oil workers their space here," Paul said. "Deadhorse is much busier than usual for this time of year."

"We were just heading down for dinner." Patience licked her throbbing lip. "We got caught in the end-of-shift rush."

"And—" Stiller hissed as Ana swiped at his cut with an alcohol pad. "That piece of shit foreman said I stepped on him. Which I didn't."

Patience's heart had jumped clear from her chest when they'd swarmed Stiller.

Ana tossed Stiller's blue streaked hair off his face. "So, you did what?"

Stiller rubbed his neck. "Told him to back the fuck off."

Patience smiled. Stiller's Boston accent and eclectic style overshadowed her southern drawl and inexperience. They were outsiders, lower forty-eighters.

"Try not to be so hostile next time." She nudged his arm.

Paul stood, his deep brown eyes looking between the two of them. "Stay out of trouble, please. I'll try smoothing things over with the foreman now, and then I'll see you in the den to go over today's data."

Stiller turned to Patience, ear and eyebrow piercings surprisingly intact. "Wasn't my elbow, was it?"

"Nah." She smiled then pressed the back of her hand to her burning split lip. "It was our new friend Mitchell's.

He was winding up for a big one."

"Thanks for trying to help me." Stiller squeezed his eyes shut as Ana closed his wound with butterfly bandages. "Even though it was a horrible idea."

Patience grabbed a bag of ice off the table and headed for the exit. "Anytime."

⅄

The fire-lit den was quiet except for Paul's incessant tapping on his laptop. Patience sighed, eyes boggling from reviewing a week's worth of data. Stiller cataloged images from the cameras attached to the belly and port of their Twin Otter plane, groaning with every tiny movement. Tattoos colored the skin above his collar and passed his sleeves, decorating his hands.

"Four different mammal species today," he said. "Not bad."

"The foreman makes five," she snickered.

Stiller inhaled mid-laugh and grabbed his ribs.

Patience had spent the entire flight to Deadhorse worrying that it all might be too much for her, especially when they landed on the icy tundra like a shuttle gliding onto the dark side of the moon. The mud had turned to ice and the temperature fell more with each day. Daylight hours plummeted.

But she had a wonderful team and Deadhorse wasn't as desolate as it sounded.

The Aurora Hotel, three stories of interconnected, pre-fabricated metal trailers, looked like nothing more than a compound from the outside. Inside it was like a dormitory. It provided a second home for the oil field workers.

Patience didn't mind the motel-like accommodations, and the staff was friendly. Eventually, she might shake the feeling of stepping on some hard-working man's boots everywhere she went. Paul had worked on a rig in his early twenties and blended in like he'd never left. Ana was of Inuit descent, a true Alaskan native.

Patience just had to ride the learning curve out and hope she didn't die.

Ana balanced Styrofoam cups in both hands and cussed under her breath. "Heads up, nerds."

Paul reclined in his seat across the coffee table. "Two creams? Five sugars?"

After a millisecond of Ana's death stare, he quietly took the cup with a gracious nod.

Ana looked toward Patience and Stiller. "Princess? City Boy?"

Stiller took a cup, muttering about his nickname.

"Hot chocolate?" Patience asked, clasping her hands together.

Ana nodded to the cup in her left hand. The Aurora Hotel wasn't a five-star resort, but the hot chocolate was damn good.

"You're the best." Patience scooted over to open a spot on the couch.

Ana parked it on the small coffee table instead and tapped Patience's knee. "Sexy. Three o'clock."

Patience jerked her head around. Frigid air slipped in behind the state trooper walking through the hotel entrance, and warm light flashed through the lobby. The door shut behind him with a quiet thud.

Forrest? Hair just a shade lighter than his snuck out from underneath his fur hat. He had the same heavy jaw but was clean-shaven. He was tall like Forrest, maybe not as broad in the shoulders, but filled out his uniform nonetheless.

Look away, Patience. Look. Away.

Yellow stripes ran down the sides of his navy-blue pants. Under his unzipped jacket, a bulletproof vest lay against his royal blue shirt. Gold emblems and patches decorated his chest and sleeves.

If she'd only gotten a chance to see Forrest in uniform.

"Something's up," Ana whispered around the rim of her cup. "Troopers don't come out here often."

"Why not?" Patience asked. The thick cloud of testosterone in the air must cook up trouble from time to time.

"North Slope Borough has a PD. Troopers out of Fairbanks handle the big stuff." Ana's gaze narrowed, and she scanned the rest of the lobby. "Maybe there's going to be a drug bust."

Fairbanks.

Patience stopped the hot liquid millimeters from her lips.

Stiller poked her shoulder. "Troopers are dicks here, too."

"That's not very nice," she whispered.

Ana kicked Stiller's feet. "Only because they have to deal with *cheechakos* like you."

Cheechako, Ana had told her it meant a newcomer to Alaska.

Patience forced Ana to make space for her on the coffee table. They kept eyes on the trooper at the registration desk. He spoke with the clerk then worked his way through the lobby, speaking with a couple in the gift shop and a group of oil workers drifting out of the cafeteria. Ana fidgeted the closer he got.

"Relax." Patience leaned into her ear. "It's not like he's a stripper for an arctic-themed bachelorette party."

Ana shot her a wide-eyed glare. "Shut up and drink your hot chocolate."

"I wonder why you're single."

Ana ran her hands down her perfect, L'Oréal commercial hair. Patience tugged on her friend's ever-present one-piece flight suit, trying to pull the front zipper down.

Ana slapped her hand. "What are you doing?"

"Trying to help your attitude." Patience liked Ana's no bullshit demeanor, but it hadn't won over anyone else.

Ana looked down at her chest covered in a blue, skin-tight, heat sealing fabric then pulled the zipper up to her neck.

Patience knew exactly what she was hiding under there. "You should just take it off."

"Be quiet. He's coming."

Paul stood to meet the trooper, propping his glasses up on his head.

"Trooper Logan Jones," the officer said.

Patience refused to swoon over his green eyes. All they did was remind her of Forrest.

"Paul Harold. I'm with the Marine Mammal Institute out of Anchorage."

"Just the man I wanted to see." Trooper Jones dug inside his coat pocket. "Run into any trouble up here?"

"That was our previous teams," Paul assured him.

"We're a fresh group. I think we'll be fine."

Paul had convinced Patience and Stiller to keep the incident with the foreman under wraps. There was no reason to jeopardize their assignment. The decision still didn't sit well with Patience.

"My partner and I are here with the governor for a few weeks." Trooper Jones handed Paul a card. "Dispatch can get a hold of us if you need anything."

"I really appreciate that." Paul shook his hand again.

Trooper Jones drifted to Patience and Ana on the coffee table. Ana took in an audible breath, and Patience couldn't help but blush for her.

"Is your team using the Twin Otter?" he asked.

Ana's voice came out in a strange squeak. "Yes."

"Saw you come in when we were getting off the Dalton." A blinding, boyish smile lit up his face. "Brought her in a little fast, didn't you?"

Patience braced herself. No one talked about Ana's flying. Ever.

Ana pushed all her hair over her shoulders. "I brought her in the way I like her."

He scribbled something on a card and handed it to Ana. "I'd be happy to show you the right way sometime."

Patience choked on a sip of hot chocolate.

Ana balled the card in her fist. "I'll remember that."

He sighed and looked down at Patience. "You. Get your coat. Outside."

Say what?

"Now." He pointed to the door.

Paul went to speak, and Trooper Jones raised his hand.

"We'll just be a minute," he said.

She shrugged at their wide-eyed stares and stood, obeying Trooper Jones's authoritative tone, and grabbed her coat from its drying spot near the fireplace hearth.

Patience walked outside into the crisp cold. Fresh ice crunched beneath her feet and fogged breath rose before her face. Lava orange burned on the horizon beneath red clouds. The colors were unreal there.

"What's your name?" he asked.

She turned away from the sky. "Patience Cline. What's going on?"

What did he want with her? It couldn't have anything to do with Forrest.

Three black Tahoes were parked between two marked trooper SUVs in front of the hotel. He led her to the first, opened the back and dropped the tailgate.

"Tell me about your lip," he said.

"Oh." She brushed her fingers across her lips.

Lie. You don't want them to scrap the survey.

"It was an accident," she said. "I slipped. I'm not used to the conditions."

Shit. That was Stiller's excuse. He was supposed to have head-butted her on accident when she'd helped him up.

He removed a camera from a black, square case. "What'd you hit your lip on?"

She eyed the hotel entrance. "A railing."

"And the guy with the blue hair? He slipped too?"

She fumbled with her gloves. "Um..."

"Hop up." He patted the tailgate. "Don't put your gloves on yet."

He took a photo of her face and the fronts and backs of her hands. "I'm a pretty accurate human lie detector, so why don't you just tell me what happened?"

Those green eyes were like magic, even if they were hard and determined. "I..."

"Logan?" Footsteps hurried toward them. "Are the rooms ready yet?"

Could it be?

Patience whipped her head around. Maybe she'd given Trooper Jones attributes of Forrest. Maybe her mind had tricked her into thinking she'd just heard him. That had to be it.

"They're working on room keys," Trooper Jones said. "They'll have the cafeteria cleared out in ten minutes."

Patience could feel it like the man had some damn tangible aura. Forrest walked into view from behind one of the Tahoes.

His lips moved, but only fog came out. In his element, in his uniform, he outshined the setting sun.

Speak, Patience. Open your mouth. Words.

"Forrest. Hi."

"You..." He rubbed his stubble covered chin. "Cut your hair."

She ran her hands through her new bob. "Yeah, I did."

Forrest took a step closer then stopped. Menace bled through his voice. "What happened?"

"Little accident." She pulled her lip between her teeth.

Trooper Jones pointed to the hotel. "Off the lobby to the left. Blue hair. Bruises and swelling on the left side of his face."

Forrest's eyes darted to the hotel entrance. His shoulders fell back, and his hands clenched into fists at his sides. "Be back in a second."

"Forrest, wait," Patience called.

He sprinted up the stairs and slipped inside before Patience could jump off the tailgate.

"He's not going to hurt him, is he?" Patience asked. "Stiller didn't do anything."

Logan eyed the hotel entrance. "Trooper Locke is pretty level-headed."

Patience twisted her gloves back and forth. "You sure about that?"

Logan's lips twitched. "We'll see."

She gawked at him. Forrest had taken off like a predator on the hunt.

Logan patted the tailgate. "I'd tell me what happened quickly if I were you."

Poor Stiller. He already got the shit beat out of him, and now Forrest was going to blame him for her injuries. The hotel doors flew open. Forrest led Stiller down the stairs and across the icy ground by a fistful of his shirt.

He jerked him to a stop in front of Patience. "Know what I'm talking about now, smart-ass?"

Stiller glared at Patience. "Did you piss this giant motherfucker off?"

Forrest wrenched his arms behind his back and cuffed him.

"Not very level today." Logan chuckled.

Patience choked on the truth, panic rising in her chest.

"I'll give you one more chance," Forrest said, "to tell me what happened."

"Goddammit." Stiller groaned, arching his back. "Fuck it. I'll tell you. I'll tell you."

Forrest eased his hold and nudged Stiller down the empty road. "That could have gone a lot easier." He cocked his head toward Logan. "Get her statement, please."

Patience climbed back onto the tailgate and stared after Forrest. He was there. In Deadhorse.

"How do you know Trooper Locke?" Trooper Jones asked.

Patience pulled her eyes from where Forrest and Stiller stood out of earshot. "We crossed paths in Chicago about a month ago."

What were the odds they'd cross paths again? In the Arctic of all places? And to think the first thing she was going to do if she survived October was call him.

"He was in Chicago for less than twenty-four hours." Trooper Jones looked down at her feet swinging under the tailgate then back up to her face.

Patience rubbed her chest then sighed. "How is he?"

Trooper Jones' lips pinched together, and he glanced at Forrest. "He's fine."

Patience nodded. "That's good. He was in a rough place."

He put his hands on his hips. "I know. He's my cousin."

She took a second to appreciate their likeness then blinked at Trooper Jones's half smile, half frown.

"What?" she asked.

He shook his head. "Nothing. Let's get back to business."

Forrest paced through the lobby past the handmade

"closed" signs in the gift shop and den. A single clerk remained at the registration desk to usher guests straight to their rooms. He didn't get a chance to see Patience before Logan sent her on her way.

Asshole.

Logan leaned against the wall beside the cafeteria doors. "She doesn't want to press any charges against the foreman."

Forrest would still make his presence known loud and clear to the man. "Neither did the kid."

"How do you know this girl, again?" Logan asked. Forrest hadn't mentioned her before. "It appears you left out the hot-piece-of-ass part of your trip to Chicago."

"Don't call her that."

He put his hands up. "You know blonde co-eds are my specialty."

"Well, I got dibs." Forrest fought the smile crossing his face.

Logan laughed. "So, she's what happened."

Forrest had been great since Chicago. Rock bottom was behind him, and every day got better and better.

"I don't know what you're talking about," he said.

"This whole time I thought you were some stone-cold son of a bitch who wasn't going to let his ex-wife get him down." Logan shook his head. "Nope. Just got some ass."

Forrest sat on the back of the couch in the den, welcoming the warm draft of air pouring down his neck. "We had a few drinks at the airport, and the flight got canceled. We had a good time."

Logan's yawn morphed into a grin. "I told you a good fuck would change your life."

"No." Forrest glanced around. "You told me to fuck everything with a pulse."

Logan paused. "That's sound advice too."

"I wish they'd hurry the hell up." Forrest checked his watch. He stood, ready to bust out of his skin if he didn't get to Patience soon.

Logan peeked into the cafeteria. "Go. I'll cover for you."

Forrest took two steps. "You're sure?"

"Yeah." He pulled his notepad out. "She's in 302. She told me to send you her way when you got a chance."

"You're an ass, you know that?"

Logan took a seat in an old rocking chair in front of the fireplace. "If you see her pilot friend, tell her I'm free for flying lessons tomorrow night."

6

Playing with Fire

By the time Forrest reached the third floor, a script had fallen into place in his head. He knew exactly what he should say and what order he would say it in.

He dumped his jacket and hat in his room then smoothed his sleeves and hat-hair down. Rushing down the main corridor of the third floor, he scrutinized every person he passed, trying to commit all their faces to memory.

When he came to room 302, he stopped, fist raised to the door.

It opened before he could knock.

Patience stepped aside wearing a white Under Armour long sleeve shirt, gray sweat pants, and furry pink socks.

Her hair stunned him again. But it wasn't the blonde locks curving under her jaw that threw him. The well-dressed, upset young woman he'd met at the airport in

Chicago had a new light to her eyes. The pink tinting her cheeks wasn't tequila induced. She'd come to the edge of the world on her own. The subtle change in her was enough for him to imagine them together a little easier.

"Come in." She smiled, bouncing on the balls of her feet.

He forced himself over the threshold.

Quiet music played in the room. The desk had an open laptop on it, the chair buried beneath her clothes. Her suitcase lay on top of the dresser beside the small television. A massive map of the Beaufort Sea hung above the bed.

She stood beside him, one sway of his body away from touching her.

"I can't believe you're here." She played with little foam circles in her hands that matched the plotted points on the map.

He tilted her head up and examined both sides of her face. "Wish I'd come sooner."

Had it been a month since he'd kissed her? His body remembered it all too well, especially his lips.

She brushed her fingers across his vest, words coming out husky and quiet. "I don't know if I can get used to the uniform, Trooper Locke."

"You mean me?" He skimmed his thumb just below her bottom lip, inhaling the faint scent of wildflowers that had led him to the suite they'd shared.

"I did fear for Stiller's life for a millisecond."

Stupid name. "He's got a mouth on him. It's no wonder he got the shit beat out of him."

Zach had won little points with Forrest. He'd put Patience in harm's way, and Forrest worried he was dumb enough to do it again. There would be no second chances.

"That's true." She leaned her head into his hand. "But that's not what I'm talking about."

She stepped back, walked over to the desk and scrolled down on her laptop, and then climbed to stand on top of the bed. After a wobble, she straightened and put a white dot on the map.

"I have this image of you in my head," she said. "And now..." She looked over her shoulder at him, chest heaving with a sigh.

He'd been down this road before. His ex hadn't married a cop, but he'd become one. The job never ended. Not even when he took his badge, or a blood-drenched uniform, off did it stop.

"It's not the same." He nodded.

"No." She steadied herself again. "There's just a lot more to think about."

Danger fueled his world. Sometimes the weight of it never left. And those were the times he needed someone, but he could never let others carry his pain.

"My job is my life." He shoved his hands in his pockets. "It can be overwhelming."

For you. And me.

She plotted another point then dropped the little white and blue circles on a pillow and walked unsteadily to the edge of the bed. The music had stopped at some point. Had it been country? R&B? What time was it?

She rested her hand on his shoulder and looked down, meeting his eyes. "Well, I'm pretty good at hauling ass when things get tough."

Forrest laughed and placed his hand on top of hers,

squeezing it. "You ride in a small twin-engine plane over the Arctic Ocean every day."

She shrugged, the corner of her mouth lifted. "Haven't quit yet."

"I don't think you're going to."

Arms locked around his neck and breasts pressed against his chin. He wrapped his arms around her body and held her close, close enough to count the beats of her heart. A giant red flag flapped inside his skull, telling him to get back to work. He was still on the job. But he couldn't walk away, not when she needed him. Not when he needed to be with her.

"How are things back home?" he whispered. "You doing okay with that?"

She'd been in a whirlwind of lies and hurt in Chicago. He could only hope some of it had fallen away.

Patience clung to Forrest. Another voicemail flashed across the screen on her phone from the desk. She'd listened to one of many when she'd come back to her room.

"He keeps calling me from Oak Island." Tears burned her eyes. "I can hear the foghorn and seagulls in the background."

"I'm sorry, Patience."

She sniffled. "I don't even care he's calling. It's just... my mom loved Oak Island."

He rubbed her back, letting the sea breeze from home find its way into her lungs.

"She would be proud of me. She would have loved to see this place."

Patience father hadn't reached out since she'd left Chicago. Brenda's secondhand account had always been enough for him.

Forrest lifted her from the bed and placed her on shaky legs. Large, steady hands pushed her hair out of her face.

"That should be all the reassurance you need." Tiny golden flecks danced around his pupils. "She loved the whales too, didn't she?"

Emotion ravaged the back of her throat. "Yeah."

Forrest kissed the top of her head. "Anything. I'm here. Doesn't matter what it is."

Patience took his hand and held it between her small ones. His calloused palms and fingers sent her right back to the bar. "I'm not much of a crutch, but if you ever need someone to cry all over your uniform..."

Forrest grinned, his eyes searching hers for something she wasn't sure she had. "You have no idea what you've done for me."

The lines in his forehead smoothed, and his jaw relaxed. The hurt she'd seen in Chicago was gone.

Patience stood on her tiptoes, and his head dipped, their faces nearly touching. Gentle lips pressed against hers, and her stomach dropped, bursting into butterflies that fluttered through her arms and legs.

She teased the seam of his mouth with her tongue, and his lips parted. Every time he gave an inch, she couldn't help but take a foot. His groan vibrated between them as she explored, tasting and reveling in the heat emanating from his entire being. She inhaled his woodsy scent over and over, using each breath to steal a little part of him. To remember him when he was gone.

Quivering legs failed her, and she slid down his body. His hands slipped over her ass and pressed against her lower back. Their lips broke apart.

He rested his forehead against hers, his chest swelling "I need to get back. If I don't leave now, I won't be able to."

Her pulse thumped between her ears. "Would that be so bad?"

The ends of her hair passed between his fingers as he ran his hands through the short strands. "No. Yes. I'll come back."

She licked her lips, noticing their throbbing for the first time. "Soon?"

He concentrated on her mouth. "As soon as I can."

Now that he was here, Chicago didn't seem so far away. If they were ever to get another chance, this was it.

She pressed her hip into his groin, a shameless attempt to get him to abandon his duty and stay with her.

"I'll hurry." His cheeks flushed to the slightest shade of pink.

She smiled, nudging his responding flesh until he pulled away and put an arms-length between them.

There was no "soon enough." What was she going to do with herself?

He removed a card from his pocket and scribbled on it. "382 is my room number. My cell, Officer Jones's, and dispatch's number are all on here if you need anything while you're in Deadhorse."

Patience took the card and held it to her chest.

He fixed an undone button on his sleeve and adjusted his vest. "I won't be long."

"I'll be here, Trooper Locke." She balled her hands up to keep them from grabbing him.

He paused at the door, and if he would've waited one second longer, she would have climbed him like a tree.

人

Patience couldn't stare at her laptop any longer, nor could she withstand the off-key singing coming from the joint bathroom between her and Ana's room. She headed down the hallway, jonesing for a bag of Bugles from the vending machine.

A sweaty, oil-stained wall of a man met her around the corner, and she stumbled backward. Mitchell, the man who'd pummeled Stiller in the stairwell, loomed over her. His ponytail was slicked back to the nape of his neck. Grease spots speckled his pants and coat.

"Where do you think you're headed?" His scraggly, gray-streaked beard shook as he spoke.

Patience inched back then peeked over her shoulder. The corridor she'd come from was empty.

"I was going to—"

"You know what I can't figure out?" he asked.

She tensed and pulled her hands into her sleeves. He didn't care what she had to say.

"What a girl like you," He flicked her hair with his finger, "is doing all the way out here."

She'd kill to have the pepper spray on her keychain. "Working. You know that."

He lowered his head, a week's worth of body odor assaulting her nose. "Do you think you're safe here?"

The women's self-defense course she'd taken her freshman year of college came back to her in a jumble of blocks and kicks. She slid her right foot back behind her.

"Why wouldn't I be? There's North Slope Borough PD and troopers."

Take the hint and leave me alone.

"North Slope Borough PD stops by once in a while. And the troopers?" He crept around her until her back was against the wall and his arm was propped above her head. "They're so deep in the governor's pocket they don't care about much else. Speaking of troopers, I hope you made Trooper Locke's little visit worthwhile."

Patience's empty stomach collapsed in on itself, and the balled fist at her ribcage fell. He'd been watching.

"I saw him go in your room," he whispered. Alcohol, prohibited at The Aurora Hotel and banned in some parts of the North Slope, tainted his breath. "He must have had a lot of questions for you."

Patience glanced down the hallway.

Please. Anyone. Come out here.

She shouldn't have left her room so late. Ana would have come with her if she'd just asked. Not even a sound from the game room overcame the silence.

"He's a friend. He was just checking on me." Her voice rose to a high pitch squeak. "We told the troopers we didn't want to press charges."

"And I don't see why any of that should change." A toothpick surfaced from his mouth. "Do we have an understanding?"

She forced the tremor racing up her body to slow down.

"It's about ten degrees outside." He looked at the emergency exit behind him, ice raining down the tiny square window. "Do you know how fast that can kill you?"

She studied his nose. Could she really force the heel of her palm into it if she had to? Could she kick him in the balls and get away before he grabbed her? Dragged her outside?

He ran his hand down the sleeve of her North Face zip up, sliding the fleece between his fingertips. The jacket wouldn't stand a chance against an Alaskan night. The cold would burn like fire.

"Depends," she stammered. "On how well equipped you are for the climate."

He chuckled. A surprisingly straight and pearly white smile lit up his face. "Accidents happen, especially to inexperienced travelers after sunset."

Patience pressed into the wall, but it wouldn't encase her, protect her from this crazy man. Why didn't he want the troopers after him?

A scream threatened to erupt from her throat. Could she prove any of this? It was her word against his. Could she survive the next few weeks if he was bent on revenge?

"As I said," she reminded him. "We're not pressing charges. We want this behind us, too."

"I'd hate to see something else happen to that pretty face if you forget that." He leaned away from her, grinning at the floor.

She nodded, water blurring her vision until she blinked the tears away.

"I think we're going to be good friends, Patience." Mitchell pushed off the wall and winked. "Bundle up. It's getting cold out."

He strolled down the hall the way she had come. Patience fell to the floor as he entered the room across from hers, her heart beating in a wild, unnatural rhythm.

Find Forrest.

Her quaking hand dug through her jacket pocket until she found his card.

Room 382

7

Night Shift

Forrest covered the last Tahoe with a tarp and ran inside from the freezing rain. Warm air pumping from the ceiling vents rushed into his airways as two fireplaces glowed in the quiet lobby.

"Trooper Locke?" Maria, the hotel manager, came from the dimly lit registration desk. "The governor's welcome banquet is all set for tomorrow evening."

Forrest could do without all the publicity stunts. He brushed ice crystals off his sleeves. "I appreciate it," he said. "Especially on such late notice. Do you think we'll have a decent turnout?"

Maria shrugged, her dark eyebrows creasing her forehead. "The oil workers aren't thrilled to see the governor, but I've never seen them turn down free food."

Signs supporting the governor's opponent in the upcoming election littered the ground outside The Aurora Hotel. Camden's assistants had made sure to slap a banner of his face across the hotel entrance to ensure it was the last thing people saw before entering. The banquet could be more than the troopers could handle if people's opinions got the best of them.

Forrest cataloged all the exits in sight, even though he'd done it a dozen times already. "Did you hear about a fight today? Between a couple of researchers and a man named Mitchell..." He removed his notepad from his breast pocket. "Mitchell Wilson?"

Sure, Forrest had concerns for the governor's safety if they had a loose cannon running around. But he couldn't stop worrying about someone else.

Maria glanced around, cautious although she was a fit, middle-aged woman with a Winchester behind the front desk. "At first, I thought the guy was just being a creep..."

Forrest dug his pen out of his pocket. "Keep going."

"There's not a lot of women in Deadhorse," she continued. "I thought he was singling them out, but he's had problems with every research team since June. I reported him to North Borough PD, but no one ever pressed charges, so they let it go. I moved Mr. Wilson to the first floor to keep a better eye on him last month."

Forrest planted his feet. Instinct begged him to scour the first floor for Mitchell. He couldn't stand a person who intimidated others just because they could. Cowards made empty threats, and he would flush this one out soon enough.

"He's just a bad apple." Maria shook her head. "Most of the oil workers are good guys just trying to do their jobs. The governor keeps cutting their paychecks, and the researchers squash every new opportunity that comes up."

"I understand their frustrations." Forrest shoved his pen and pad back in his pocket. "But Mr. Wilson may need to find lodging elsewhere during his work rotations in Deadhorse. I'll speak with him. Let me know of any more trouble, would you?"

Logan's voice came over the radio. "Deadhorse 171 to 520."

Forrest shook Maria's hand and headed down the main corridor. "Go ahead, 171."

"I've got a ten-thirty-seven up here," Logan said. "What's your twenty?"

Suspicious person. Forrest checked his back. Nothing but silence followed him.

"Lobby." Forrest headed for the east stairwell, eyeing all doors and exits. "I'm headed up."

"Black jacket. Black pants."

"Anything else?" He took the stairs two at a time, forcing his cold body to come alive. Logan never called for backup.

Forrest rested his hand on his gun at the third-floor platform, hoping his cousin would wait for his arrival to approach the suspect.

"Blonde. Blue eyes," Logan said. "About 5'3." Maybe 5'4."

Forrest's hand fell from his hip. "Really, Jones?"

"She says 5'4," but I'm not buying it."

Forrest tempered the smile shooting across his face and opened the door.

Patience stood back from Logan, arms crossed tightly across her chest. She bounced on the balls of her feet. His stomach tensed at her tight-lipped smile.

"Are you all right?" he blurted.

She nodded and pointed to his room. "Can we talk?"

He checked his watch. "Of course. It's time for us to call it a night, anyway." He unlocked his room, unable to keep from touching her as she rushed to his side. "Go on in. I need to talk to Trooper Jones for a second."

Her doe eyes glistened. "I'm sorry I just showed up. I should have called. I know you said you'd come by."

He shook his head. "It's fine. I'll be right in."

Logan whistled at the closed door and leaned back against the hallway wall. He grinned.

"I don't want to hear it." Forrest turned his flushed face away.

"Hey, she came back for more." Logan slapped him on the shoulder. "Congrats, man."

"Listen." Forrest scrubbed his face and rubbed his eyes. "I talked to the hotel manager. Our guy, Mitchell, has had run-ins with all of the teams from the marine institute."

Logan's brows shot up. "Headquarters said he's got a decade of assaults and was a suspect in a missing person's case last year."

Forrest couldn't stand idle with this guy around. Not with Patience in the crosshairs. "We need to remove him."

Tensions would only rise as the governor's campaign commenced. Forrest had to be proactive not to just protect the man he was assigned to, but to keep Patience, her team, and the community safe.

Logan nodded. "Let me know how you want to handle this guy. I'll be right behind you."

Forrest didn't doubt it. "If we can't get a hold of

him first thing in the morning, we'll see him when the governor tours the rigs and have a little chat."

"I like chats." Logan scanned the hallway then smirked. "Try to get some sleep tonight, all right?"

Forrest waved him off. He took a minute by himself, trying to figure what kind of line he would be crossing by entering his own room.

In every roundabout way he could, he tried not to label Patience a victim. For her benefit and his own. Altercations between Alaskans and outsiders happened all the time, and she could've just been in the wrong place at the wrong time. Or she'd been sought out, and if charges ever came to light, they may not stand if Forrest was compromised, especially if he took things out of the law and into his own hands. Just the thought of someone watching her, putting their hands on her...

How would he enforce the law if his emotions were calling the shots? Logan operated that way. Forrest couldn't afford to.

He pushed the door open, and Patience hit him like a wall of pillows.

"Honey." He rested his head on top of hers and wrapped his arms around her shoulders. "I told you I'd come see you." His gut twisted and turned. "You're sure you're all right?"

"I'm...I..." She let out a massive sigh. "I just couldn't wait."

He scanned her face before she pulled his head down. Warm lips met his cool ones, matching the heat of her hands on his wind-burned cheeks.

Do your job, Forrest.

"Listen," he mumbled, unable to stop from kissing

her back. "Talk. We need to talk first."

Strawberry filled his nose and coated his tongue as her lip balm dissolved between their mouths.

"No." She sucked on his bottom lip long and hard.

He melted just a little. Just enough to pull her closer, but not enough to forget what he needed to say. If he didn't get the words out soon, he worried he never would.

"We need to get on the same page, Patience." *I can't keep everyone in line when all I can think about is you.* "I'm spread thin here."

"What are you saying?" She slid the zipper of his jacket down.

"I need to ask you some questions. I have concerns about your safety." *I need to handle this appropriately.* "Then..." He rolled his shoulders, itching to get out of his uniform. "I need to take a shower and get a good night's sleep."

I need to control the situation.

"Here's the problem," she said, dragging both her hands through her hair. "I don't want to talk right now." Her fingers skimmed down her neck and over her chest.

Every cell in his body beckoned to her call. "Please. I'm on the job, Patience."

I can't be distracted. Not until you're safe.

"You weren't worried about your job earlier. C'mon, Forrest. A little distraction is just what you need." Her words fell over him like a sweet promise.

He couldn't stop his thumb from caressing her bruised lip. "We need to talk about Mitchell. He's dangerous."

Her gaze drifted away, the bedside table lamp glowing in her pupils. "I don't want to talk about Mitchell."

Forrest waited for her to re-establish eye contact with him.

It never happened.

"Patience?"

"I don't want to talk about him." She plopped down on the edge of the bed, her focus glued to the floor.

One step away from pulling his pen and notepad out of his pocket, he took the chair from the room's small desk and sat down.

"Did Mitchell make contact with you any time before or after the altercation today?" he asked.

She shook her head no and smoothed the comforter on the bed.

Look at me and stop fidgeting so I know you're not lying.

"He hasn't approached you? Has anyone else?"

She untangled the telephone cord on the nightstand. "No."

He couldn't soften his deep, monotone words. "Mitchell has a history of violence."

Patience stilled. Her hand was an inch from the crooked lampshade disrupting the flow of light into the room.

Forrest couldn't help himself as she sucked in her bruised bottom lip. "If he so much as speaks to you—"

"Don't hound him." Her eyes finally met his. "I don't need any more trouble, Forrest. Okay?"

Heat consumed the last bit of cold that had numbed his fingers. He flexed them, trying to break the tension building in the muscles of his forearms. The desperation in her stare made it so much harder.

"I have a few more weeks to do my job." She tucked

her hair behind both ears. "The drillers think we're trying to take money from them and there's no changing that."

"In your own words," Anger blazed up his back, "it's possible Mitchell was sending a message when he busted up your friend's face?"

Her glare cut across the room and set him back in his seat. "Don't put words in my mouth," she said. "It was an accident, and it's been resolved."

He pointed at her, struggling to keep himself in check. "And the incidents he's had with all your other teams? Those accidents too?"

She ran her hands down her thighs and gripped the loose denim at her knees. "He's trying to scare us. Just leave it alone, Forrest."

He rose to his feet and put the chair away as calmly as he could. Would he delve so deep if it was someone else? Wouldn't he just tell their team leader to keep an eye on his people and monitor the peace? They were in the Arctic. Backup was hundreds of miles away. It was too easy for someone to get hurt, especially when everyone was on edge in the cramped, wintry conditions. Forrest knew better.

He rolled his shoulders, needing to get out of his uniform and wash the day off. "I'm not trying to put words in your mouth. I just care about you." *Did he have to say that?* "I'm getting in the shower. Then maybe we can try this again."

Maybe you'll listen to me.

He couldn't look at her as he dumped his coat over the desk and grabbed a long sleeve shirt and sweatpants from his suitcase.

His job came first. Always had and always would.

In the bathroom the dry sink stared back at him as he braced himself over it, listening, waiting to hear Patience leave. He couldn't stop her, trap her. Keep her in his reach even if it was the safest place for her to be.

When the water sputtered from the showerhead and hit his shoulders, it was her chance to slip out. It'd been easy enough for her the first time.

"Forrest?"

His head whipped up at the hard edge tracing every letter of his name. Patience stood in the bathroom doorway, hair springing out in every direction on top of her head. He kept his eyes on her over the shower door and leaned his back against the cool, droplet covered shower wall.

She couldn't cross her arms any tighter. "You're not the only one here with a job to do."

But I call the shots.

She shook a little. "I knew it wasn't going to be easy here."

He ran his hand over his damp hair. "I'm not trying to make it easier for you. I'm just trying to make sure you get home safe."

He paused halfway into the waterfall. What happened after Deadhorse? Would it be goodbye again? Would she say to hell with it all and go back east?

He shifted his achy legs, confused how he could miss someone he hardly even knew.

"I'm going to do what I came here for." Her arms shot straight to her sides, her hands in fists. "I may never get another opportunity like this."

I may never meet someone like you again.

Keeping her close satisfied the cop and the man in him. The cop would be able to let her go when the danger passed. The man...

"There is no choice for me, Patience." He turned up the hot water. "I'm going to do everything in my power to keep you safe, whether you like it or not."

"Why?" Her stance fell apart, and she sagged against the bathroom wall. Her bottom lip quivered.

Please don't cry.

"That's just who I am." He snatched a bottle of body wash from the shower ledge and lathered some between his hands. He'd always had a hard time letting go. It made him a persistent investigator. Made him follow through until he found the ugly or the beautiful in people.

"I can do this job." She stared at the ceiling. "I can handle this."

He braced himself against the shower wall. "Honey, I never said you couldn't."

She'd been surprising him since the moment he met her and didn't expect her to stop.

Her gaze fell to the floor, and he couldn't stand the space between them.

No matter how heavy the responsibility of his badge weighed on his shoulders, he couldn't compartmentalize the way he needed to with Patience. Tunnel vision erased the big picture where he was a state trooper, and she was a witness, and possibly a victim. The girl who had seduced him in Chicago and licked his wounds now had the potential to give him new ones. It didn't scare him as it should. For some reason, it didn't scare him at all.

8

Like the Rain

Green eyes seemed to see through thick, wet lashes and beyond Patience's façade. She didn't have to be alone here. Forrest was the buffer against the ice, the people, and all the unknown. He was as strong as the frontier was wild.

Tell him you're scared. Tell him everything.

"I'm sorry I barged in." She couldn't stand to leave. She couldn't stand lying to him again.

If Mitchell had harassed every research team, then the fight with Stiller had been no accident. Patience had to buck up and get through this just how the other teams had.

It's all a part of the job. Isn't it?

"Maybe tomorrow..."

You'll kiss me again. You'll make everything disappear.

He licked away a drop of water clinging to his lip. "I

don't want you to leave."

"I don't want to lie to you." The words flew from her mouth. "God, um..."

Patience steadied herself, keeping her head above the sea of worry and fear long enough to take a few breaths.

Nothing but splattering water answered her back. She couldn't read his face over the paned glass. Did he look at everyone that way? With no judgment, just expectation?

"Mitchell cornered me in the hallway." The words echoed in her mind. "He doesn't want you after him."

The water shut off.

"Did he threaten you?" Forrest's voice was loud, but level.

Panic bled into her words. "He said accidents can happen after sunset."

There. She'd said it.

The fogged door slid open and banged against the wall. Forrest whipped a towel off the rack as he climbed out. A split-second glimpse of his entire body threw her back to Chicago.

Flashbacks of his strong, thick thighs against the backs of hers sent her pulse into double time. It was as if she'd forgotten how massive he was until he was naked. Natural and untouched, he radiated so much more power than he did when in uniform.

"Don't leave this room," he ordered. "Logan's next door if I'm gone long."

Patience stepped into his path and put her hands up. Little streams of water cut paths through the dark hair across his chest. She followed them down the tensed ripples of his stomach.

"Wait. Let's not murder anyone tonight."

If he fell apart, she sure as hell didn't stand a chance. Logan had said Forrest was level-headed, and she would have sworn that about him after they'd met.

He took her face in his damp hands. "If something happens to you, it's bad for everybody. Do you understand that?"

She couldn't look away from his eyes even if she tried. "Uh-huh."

"It's bad for your boss who told you to lie about the fight. It's bad for the marine institute who knew there was trouble in Deadhorse. And it's bad for me."

Bad for him?

His hands balled into fists and fell to his sides. "I can't wait for the law to catch up to Mitchell, and there's no one who can stop me from protecting you. Let me through."

Patience soaked up his words like they were some kind of love-declaring violent poetry.

"Just stay with me." She needed him back to his cool, collected self. If he could brush this off, she could too. "I don't want to be alone."

I don't want you to make a mistake because of me.

Forrest put his hands on the back of his head, breathing so deep and quick she worried he was only amping himself up. In the shadow of his wingspan, she tried not to imagine the pain he could inflict on someone. She hadn't even mentioned Mitchell roomed across the hall from her yet.

He turned to the mirror, reflection frozen. She'd asked him to be someone he wasn't, to put the badge down for her sake. Guilt climbed up her throat.

He turned back to her, droplets falling from his spiked hair as he dragged his hands through it. "The morning. I'll wait until the morning."

Gravity bore down a little easier on Patience.

The rigid stance he'd taken eased, and he held his arms out. "Come here."

She slammed against him, sticking to his moist skin.

An immeasurable beat thumped against her ear. Steady. Unwavering. She fed off it, mimicking the strength in hopes of convincing herself everything was going to be fine. But no matter how hard she held him, no matter how hell-bent on her safety he was, she needed to escape.

There was only one place she wanted to be.

The window had been cool on her back, his hands hot on her skin. The night had been alive with lights, and the morning too distant to feel. She'd left one world behind and was on the precipice of another.

"Take me back to Chicago," she whispered.

He stroked her hair. "When?"

"Now."

She looked up into his thoughtful eyes, and he shook his head.

"No." He moved her hands behind his neck. "We're here now."

Where exactly were they? In the land of friends? Opportunists? She couldn't stop the strange feeling swirling in the pit of her stomach that they'd taken some invisible step. A step she stood on with tiptoes, trying her damnedest to get her mouth closer to his.

He dipped his head and whispered, "I probably

shouldn't be saying this, but I don't want to let this second chance slip by."

The words fed a need that had gotten unexpectedly hungry. "I don't want you to either."

He walked her backward into the bedroom. "I just need you to be honest with me. Always."

Other people's lies had thrown them into each other's arms in the first place. Her running from her past, and him hiding from his future.

"I'm sorry." She tilted her face up, waiting for that kiss. "I—"

Forrest picked her up and wrapped her legs around his hips, a cloud of arousal softening his face and parting his lips.

"It's okay," he murmured. "I'm going to keep you safe."

His lips skimmed along her jawline, and the seconds stopped as she breathed him in. They were in their own little snow globe at the top of the world.

Forrest had been right. They didn't need to go back to Chicago.

A fleeting kiss landed on the corner of her mouth, and her lips chased his, anticipation dissolving the pain from her split lip. She coaxed Forrest's mouth back to hers, and he dove in at the invitation. His tongue met hers with deft strokes that made her body light but her eyes heavy.

He spun them around and sat on the edge of the bed, the white towel around his hips gone. Patience panted softly in his lap, trying to help him tear her jacket away. His hands were already climbing up her back and unhooking her bra when her shirt hit the floor.

Like the tide coming in, anticipation washed down her body, and she wanted nothing more than for Forrest to feel it. To know the place she was slipping into with him.

λ

Forrest buried his face in Patience's bare chest. The warmth pouring off her filled his lungs with a breath so deep he was sure the earth had stopped spinning.

She'd barely uttered the words that someone meant her harm, and he'd rushed to the edge of his control. If he thought about his actions longer than a second, he'd bet it was just an excuse to get closer to her. Another tie to Patience to make. Another reason to toss his own damn advice out the window.

Just the sight of her flushed skin his mouth left behind as he travelled across the swell of her breasts made anything wrong feel right. He ran his hands up the denim stretched atop her thighs and dug his fingers in as deep as the ones she was pressing into his shoulders.

His cock ached and pulsed like it remembered what Patience could do to him. Memories that filled his dreams bled into reality, and he groaned, moving his lips to her neck.

Her lips grazed the top of his ear and flowery shampoo filled his nose as he undid her jeans. The backs of his hands skimmed her thin cotton underwear and he cupped her ass. His fingers rubbed against a strangely textured area and he paused as he traced the square patch with his thumb.

"This what I think it is?" he asked.

Patience's mouth pulled away from his neck and he

regretted it instantly. Every nerve in his body stood on edge, waiting for the next touch.

"Didn't think I'd remember to take a pill every day out here."

He never thought to bring protection to the Arctic. "When you switched birth controls did you have to get..."

She nodded. "I'm good. Did you get checked after you found out about you-know-who?"

"First thing I did." He swallowed. It had been a small victory. "I'm good."

He slid his hands up her lower back, a realization hitting him so hard he couldn't stop his insides from quivering. "You're the only person I've been with since."

A quiet purr came from Patience, and she threaded her fingers through his hair. Tingles spread from Forrest's scalp all the way down his spine. His mind reached for a faraway place where she was his forever. Where the only hands that would touch her would be his, and the only man that would ever be inside her was him.

Patience forced him to lie back onto the bed. He propped himself up on his elbows to watch her shimmy off the rest of her clothes. Her soft, now paler curves promised the world and so much more as she climbed on top of him.

When her first kiss hit his chest, every muscle in his body tensed. Patience's gaze drifted up to his face, and her sly smile sent a rush of heat to his face. He tried to relax as she drifted down his torso, tongue snaking out between her lips to scorch his skin.

A hard nipple grazed his erection and he ground his teeth, the tease morphing into a moment of pain he wasn't sure he could take. She grabbed the base of his cock and settled on her knees between his legs. The pent-up breath in his lungs grew tighter as her ass lifted, and her head dipped.

Patience's looked up before she took the tip into her mouth. Forrest's chest collapsed, thoughts melting with the hot, delicious swirls of her tongue around his swollen head. He brushed back the hair falling into her face, unable to fight the groan vibrating through his chest.

The pull of her mouth brought him in deeper—a soft, sinful pressure enveloping his length until her lips bumped her hand over and over.

A warm sea of pleasure swept him up, making his hips lift and his hand reach for hers splayed across his stomach. Every knock against the back of her throat brought a wave of bliss he couldn't navigate, only ride.

She pulled away in one slow motion, her half-lidded eyes hungry and her lips glistening. An overwhelming urge to reach for her hit him. Sweat broke out on the back of his neck and forehead as she crawled up his body. The tiniest brushes of her skin on his accelerated a fire he desperately tried to cool.

Don't flip her over. Let her take the reins.

She hovered above him and reached between their bodies. Slow and easy, she guided him to her entrance, rubbing the head in the wetness of her folds before sliding it gently inside.

Forrest could die at the kiss of heat and worried he might as she sank slowly towards him. A moan escaped him as her tight, silky walls molded around his girth. He soaked up the quiet sounds on the tail end of her breaths, loving the response of her body to his and the rosiness of her cheeks as she seated herself on him.

A dangerous feeling surfaced, and it scared him how much he wanted to hold on to it. Patience made it easy for him to embrace it, though, leaning against his chest for leverage and grinding her pelvis against his seamlessly. There was nothing that could take him away from this moment. An overwhelming need burned through his veins, and his hands desperately tried to memorize the raw beauty riding him, bearing down on him with an unbelievable force as time dissipated.

When she leaned back and braced her arms against his thighs, he slid his thumb over her glistening, spread pussy, grazing the smooth hood of her swollen clit. The intoxicating rhythm rolling over her breasts and torso moved through him as he massaged the hot bud in a purposeful circle.

Irresistible depths swallowed his cock until his balls tightened and he bucked. Tension snapped as her head fell back, and an unbearable pressure squeezed him with a blue-flamed intensity that rocked his entire being.

He spilled inside of her, gripping her milking hips with his hands and biting back a shout. She crumbled, and he caught her in a breathless kiss, her body quaking. Lingering spasms rippled through her, and he held her until they stopped, their heaving chests falling into unison.

"Remember in Seattle," Patience said, resting her face against his shoulder, words coming out in a breathy whisper, "when you told me to call you when I was ready?"

Their misaligned lives had tried to come together then. They didn't fit yet, but he didn't care. He wanted it all no matter where the pieces fell.

He rolled her onto her back, pulled himself free, and lay by her side. "Of course, I do."

She caressed his cheek, thumb gliding over his stubble. "Are you ready?"

9

Into the Ocean

Patience nestled into Forrest's chest as they lie in the quiet of the morning. He'd slept soundly while she'd lain awake, wondering if Mitchell was looking for her. The wind had whistled for hours, and ice had snuck onto the glass of the room's windowpane.

In the Arctic's ever-prevalent darkness, she gripped Forrest and took a deep breath. "There's something else I need to tell you about Mitchell."

Forrest's hand stopped mid-pass through her hair. "What?"

"After he threatened me in the hallway, he went into the room across from mine."

Forrest didn't move. Didn't speak.

"I had no idea he was staying there." She propped herself up on her elbow and tried to gauge his mood. For a split second, his face hardened.

"When I told you, I was ready for *us*, I meant it," he

said. "Not telling me something is just as good as lying."

Oh no. She wasn't a speeder at a traffic stop. The badge didn't make decisions for her.

"Keeping you from doing something you might regret was what I was doing." She wasn't going to stand in the background of another relationship. Not this one.

Forrest looked away and nodded. "Fair enough."

He slipped from the bed, and she could feel the heaviness of the room as he moved through it. She got up and put her clothes on as he put his uniform on piece by piece, slowly morphing into a man that meant nothing but business.

His eyes locked on his reflection in the mirror, he wedged his phone between his shoulder and ear. Whatever jargon he and Logan muttered back and forth was discreet enough to keep her out of the loop. Their short conversation ended as Forrest finished buttoning his sleeve cuffs.

"I'll take you to your room, make sure it's safe. Then I'm going to find Mitchell."

She swallowed, but the dread wouldn't move down her throat. When Mitchell had said he didn't want the troopers after him, all she'd been able to think about was her safety. Now she was doing exactly what he told her not to, but she wouldn't be in his path this morning. It would be Forrest.

Logan entered the hallway at the same time they did. In lieu of a uniform, he wore only low-slung pajama pants. Tousled dark hair, lean cuts of muscle, and hooded eyes were all overshadowed by the Glock in his hand. He handed it to Forrest.

"Let me know when you locate him," he said.

Goosebumps spilled across Patience's skin at the growl in his voice. She scanned the hallway for other hotel guests—empty.

Forrest tucked the firearm into the back of his pants. "Will do."

Logan nodded and slipped back inside his room.

Her stomach rolled.

She walked alongside Forrest to her room, unsure how close her arm was allowed to swing to his. "Why doesn't Logan just go with you instead of giving you his weapon?"

He drifted closer to her, pressing his hand gently against her lower back. "Do you have any experience with handguns?"

"My brother gave me a .40 caliber Glock for Christmas a few years ago. It's pink camo. He made sure I got my concealed weapons permit before he left." If she hadn't been in such a hurry when she left North Carolina, she would have brought it. "Still, I don't think you should go by—"

"Good." Forrest smirked. "You shouldn't have any problem with this. It's Logan's personal weapon."

It was for her? Patience shook her head even though her feet moved her forward. Ever since her brother left for his first deployment, she'd had her concealed weapons' permit. He'd gone to the classes with her and taken her to the shooting range on the weekends. It unnerved her more than any rifle she'd sat behind as a kid. Handguns were meant for protection, not sport.

At her room, Forrest took the key from her frozen hand and entered first. Satisfied, he led her inside, glanced around the small space, and closed the door.

"Check on Ana for me, please."

"She's going to kill me if I wake her up." Patience tiptoed into their shared bathroom and grasped the knob to Ana's room. She twisted it silently, the glow from her room shining across the body snoring beneath a pile of blankets.

Pulling the door closed, she backpedaled out of the bathroom and pressed her finger to her lips. Forrest nodded, and then his head jerked around. The whirling of an electric lock opening cut through the air.

The door opened, and Forrest shoved Patience behind him, the sound of his weapon sliding from its holster slicing through the air.

Forrest grabbed his radio. "Ten-sixty-nine."

Mitchell stood in the doorway, his scraggily-haired jaw falling open. "Fuck."

Patience gripped the back of Forrest's vest, pulse hammering through her skull as she looked under his extended arm.

"Hands up," Forrest's command boomed across the room.

Mitchell's arms shot up. "I can explain." His eyes shifted from left to right.

"Don't move." Forrest stepped purposely toward him, pulling Patience by her death grip "Don't give me a reason to kill you."

Mitchell stared at the ground, and his chest heaved. Patience gasped when his arms fell and he darted back into the hall. Before Forrest could reach the door, Mitchell was shuffling back to the room, his eyes pinched closed and his head wrenched to the side.

Logan pressed the barrel of a gun to his temple.

"You've already given me enough reason."

Patience stood idle, hair sticking to the sweat on the back of her neck.

Forrest kept his back to her, never taking his gaze away from Mitchell. "Go to Ana's room, Patience. Now."

Rage and fear swirled through Logan. The "what ifs" wouldn't stop battering his mind.

We got him. She's okay.

Forrest backed into the room. "Walk."

Logan nudged Mitchell forward and closed the door behind them.

"I swear." Water filled Mitchell's eyes. "I wasn't going to hurt her."

Forrest came forward and searched him, throwing a room key and flash drive he'd found in his pocket onto the floor. Logan refused to drop his weapon after Forrest cuffed him. Fuck protocol. He was going to scare the piss out of this motherfucker then beat the ever-loving shit out of him.

Forrest spun Mitchell around, and for the first time, Logan thought his cousin might set the badge aside. He lowered his head to stare the foreman in the eye, neutrality lost to a vengeful hatred Logan had never seen before.

"Why her?" Forrest asked.

"I was just going to apologize." Mitchell's mouth quivered.

Logan scoffed and cracked his neck. "That's why you let yourself into a young woman's room at five o'clock in the morning? To say sorry?"

Every crime scene stayed with him no matter how hard he tried to forget them. It didn't matter what Mitchell's intentions were. It never would.

"I didn't do anything," Mitchell whispered.

"You threatened her last night." Forrest bit out the words. "You've threatened every research team from the marine institute since they got here. Why?"

Logan rose onto the balls of his feet. Questions. Too many questions. "I'm not going to stop. Even after I beat the fucking answers out of you."

Mitchell strained his neck away from Logan. "I wasn't going to hurt her. Just scare her."

Forrest's stare met Logan's for the first time. For once, his cousin might let him unload his anger on this deserving piece of shit. It was right there, waiting.

Logan flipped his gun around to hold the barrel and Mitchell jumped. "Don't like scientists? Is that it?"

Logan hated men who intimidated women. Even if the researchers threatened the growth of drilling in Alaska, it didn't constitute this.

Mitchell looked between the two of them. "Just listen to me for a second. I'm not the one in charge here."

Logan didn't want to listen, but Mitchell's claim cooled his rage. "What?"

Mitchell's raised palms dropped a little. "I'm just doing my job."

Forrest rolled his shoulders and shook his head at Logan. They should have known. They both should have sensed something was wrong. Deadhorse was no place for a polished politician.

"Who do you work for?" Forrest demanded.

Mitchell gulped. "The same man you do."

Logan's skin burned. They were all in deep shit. Them, Patience, the whales, probably Mitchell too.

"What were you going to do to her?" Forrest crossed his arms and studied the bound man.

"The flash drive." Mitchell nodded toward Patience's laptop on the desk. "I couldn't break through her firewalls last night. I need her to install a program that'll allow us remote access to her computer."

Logan could feel Forrest's stare, but he wouldn't look at him. They were on dangerous ground. The governor was using Mitchell to do his dirty work.

"You're trying to make sure the Beaufort is open for drilling." Forrest bit his bottom lip. "How do you plan on getting away with that?"

Mitchell inched back. "She's got to manipulate the data herself. He'll make her an accomplice so she can't turn on him. I tried to keep you out of it. It's not personal, Forrest. Just business. I had no idea you knew the girl."

Logan shot his partner a sideways glance. They were going to use Patience. The safest route for everyone was to do the governor's bidding. He could take their badges, her career, or worse.

They'd brought along the wrong state trooper to cover up a conspiracy on the campaign trail, though.

"You're never going to see Patience again," Forrest promised.

$$\Lambda$$

Patience made small tears along the edge of the flyer that had slipped beneath Ana's door. Murmurs, some louder than others, were all that had come from her room. Well, other than a muffled scream and some thumps.

Even though Ana had been sound asleep when Patience came into her room, she was now wide awake with an ear against the bathroom door. "I think they're done with their *interview*."

"You think the institute is going to pull us?" Patience tucked her knees to her chest as she sat on the room's only chair.

Ana pulled her hair into a messy bun on top of her head and snatched the flyer. "I could miss this bullshit banquet for the governor tonight."

And just like that, her biggest opportunity was squashed by a lunatic. "I think I'm going to be sick."

"Pay..." Ana sat on the end of the bed. "Maybe if the troopers say we're safe, they'll let us stay. But someone came into your room. Threatened you. I'm a tough bitch, but that's—"

"We need to stay." Patience rubbed her stomach. "Complete the survey."

They were all safer with Mitchell gone, but she couldn't shake the feeling that she'd just stirred up an even bigger shit-storm. If he'd never spotted her with Forrest, this wouldn't have even happened. Mitchell had been watching her closely, though—too close. She wanted to run. Do what she always did. But she needed to be level-headed, professional.

Snowflakes drifted past her window. The frigid cold was coming. Could she really make it out there?

A tap came from the bathroom door, and Patience caught herself before she fell out of the desk chair.

Ana let Forrest in, and just the sight of him made her throat constrict with emotion. He knelt in front of her and brushed her cheek with his thumb. A grimace broke up the hard lines of his face.

"We're arranging transport for Mitchell to the jail in Barrow. Honey, I have to call the institute. I'm sorry, but I have to get you out of Deadhorse."

"Even with Mitchell gone?" she whispered.

He took her hand. "It's not safe here."

She blinked back the welling tears and rubbed her aching chest. "Are you okay? I heard—"

"Don't you worry about me. I'm fine." He cupped her cheek and wiped away another rogue tear. "Just go about your day as normal. Stay close to your team. I'll see you tonight."

She squeezed his hand and forced a smile.

Forrest stood, kissed the top of her head, and whispered, "It's in the nightstand."

10

Speechless

Patience spent the day glued to her teams' side. Even on the plane, as they cruised above the Beaufort, she'd huddled close to Stiller. The crisp air had gotten sharper and the sea angrier overnight. By the time they'd landed back in Deadhorse, she was numb, her spirit broken. It would all be for nothing. Their whale counts for October would be accepted as is or rejected due to incompletion. The data straddled a delicate line when it came to determining if whale populations were too fragile to allow offshore drilling in the Beaufort Sea. Appeals and petitions would be inevitable from both sides—those trying to protect the whales and those looking for black gold.

Ana wrapped her arm around Patience's shoulder as they stood on the outskirts of the crowded banquet. "Stop worrying about things you can't control."

Patience sipped a cup of ginger ale, the noise of

the crowd mixing with her thoughts and threatening to swallow her whole. "Then you stop pulling on your sweater."

Ana squirmed in the borrowed cashmere; her typical bitch face softened by the coral threads. Patience forgot what it was like to have girlfriends. When she met Chris, she'd dumped them all. Even though they mostly bickered, she liked bickering with Ana. They didn't delve into hair and fashion as much as Patience wanted too, but they talked boys, planes, and whales.

"I look ridiculous," Ana muttered.

"You look lovely."

A wave of testosterone swelled through the crowd as the governor appeared. The suits following him dispersed through the throng, forcing smiles and handshakes on the oil workers. Most ignored the politician and his aides, piling their plates at the cafeteria buffet and meeting in their own groups of friends.

"Since when does "lovely" get you anywhere?" Ana asked.

Patience did a double-take of the ice sculpture on display by the gift shop. Paul had caught the artist at work and paid him two hundred bucks to turn the intended howling wolf into a breaching Orca. Trooper Jones emerged from behind it, shaking his head.

Patience still couldn't shake his uncanny resemblance to Forrest. " "Lovely" might get you some of that."

Ana's caramel skin reddened, and she turned around. Patience blushed as Logan's wanton gaze traveled up and down Ana's back. The damn outfit was supposed to be for *Ana's* confidence.

"I'd get him to help you with that sweater before we

head home," Patience whispered.

"Stop it." Ana tightened the back of her diamond stud earring. "Is he coming over?"

"Yep." Patience elbowed her friend's side. "See you later."

Logan's reassuring smile looked just like Forest's and took the edge off of her nerves. He caught her elbow just as they passed each other. "Transport came through. Forrest will be here soon."

"Thank you." She breathed easy for the first time in hours and headed toward the drink station.

Patience dropped three ice cubes into her cup. She was alone. Frozen water clattered between her hands, and she gripped the cup tighter.

Calm down. Mitchell's gone. Mingle. Don't be the weirdo in the corner.

"Are there any Cokes left?"

Patience spun into a sky-blue dress shirt with the sleeves rolled to the elbows. She managed to catch her flying ice cubes before they bounced against the cologne-drenched stranger.

"Whoa, sweetheart. Are you all right?"

She took a deep breath, steadied by his grasp, and lifted her head. The governor of Alaska smiled an easy, well-practiced smile. His chestnut hair matched his eyes and skin like a Ken doll's. If he had gray, he was covering it up with a nice dye job. Patience guessed him to be around her father's age but in much better shape.

"Yes. I'm sorry. I think there are some."

He scooped a cup of ice and grabbed a can. "You

must be Patience."

She tried to control whatever god-awful face she must be making. "How do you know my name?"

He poured soda into his cup. "I just had a chat with Paul. He said you were the one to speak to about the Beaufort Sea survey this year. I may not be young like you anymore, but I'm still just as passionate about my work."

Did Paul dump the governor on her? Or did he really think she was so passionate she should be the voice of their research? She dreaded the look on his face when the institute scrapped the survey. She sipped on the melting ice in her cup. Where the fuck was Forrest?

"What would you like to know?" she asked.

"Everything." He laughed and motioned to the table behind them. "I think the hot chocolate is at the dessert table if you're done with your ice."

A strange twinge snuck across her chest. How did he know she liked hot chocolate? How paranoid was she? Whether she had a job tomorrow or not, if she ever had a chance to talk to somebody with power about Alaska's marine mammals, this was it.

$$\bigwedge$$

Logan stole another glance at Ana. Awkward silences weren't really his thing.

"So, you like it up here?" he asked.

Her frown deepened. "It's eight below. Nobody likes it up here."

The reddish-orange sweater against her brown-sugar skin called to him like a beacon in the darkness. It almost drowned out her shitty attitude. Almost.

"I just thought..."

"What? That I left my *amauti* and harpoon at home?"

He turned to get a good look at her face. She kept scanning the bustling room, borderline stone-faced, borderline pissed the hell off. If she wanted to be that way, it was cool by him. But he didn't buy it for a second.

"I like a caribou parka and whaling just as much as the next person." He laughed and scratched his head. "I guess I'll see you around."

A gentle hand touched his arm. "Wait," she said.

Hook, line, and sinker. He stared at her piano fingers and bright red nails on his jacket surprised such delicate things maintained and flew planes.

"That was rude of me." Her hand fell away.

A couple of compliments and he should be golden. Oh, how he loved sweet victory.

"It's my fault. I figured an Inuit pilot would be invaluable for an MMO survey team in the Arctic," His face grew hotter as her eyes grew wider, "but you may not even be Inuit. And I should probably stop putting my foot in my mouth."

It took a heart-pounding second, but she cracked a little smile. "I might be Inuit."

"That's good." He pressed his palm against the beating in his chest. "And it wouldn't kill you to smile more. I mean, it might kill me, but..."

Whoa, buddy. Slow down. You got this.

"Are you all right?"

She leaned into him, chocolate hair swooshing over her shoulder and big brown eyes looking for his soul. He'd seen plenty of beautiful women, but his body was convinced it had found something new and inched closer.

"No." He stilled as her breasts grazed him with her deep breaths. "Just off my game."

Did I really just admit that?

"What game?" Her husky voice sent chills down his arms.

"I think you're trying to make a joke," he murmured. "Leave the jokes to me."

"But you're not funny." She tilted her head, her focus zeroing in on his mouth.

"Are you kidding?" He skimmed his fingers down the back of her hand. "I'm hilarious."

She rose onto her tiptoes, but he took his time lowering down to meet her. It may be the only time she ever wanted him, and it felt better than it should.

"Hey, Ana," A man's voice called out from somewhere behind Logan.

Logan jerked backward and bumped into the man behind him.

Stiller burst through the crowd, a small console in his hand. "I'm stuck on another level. Can you beat it for me?"

Ana grabbed at her shoulders like she was pulling at an imaginary jacket then crossed her arms tightly across her chest. "What are you talking about?"

Logan kept his mouth pinned shut, hiding his breathlessness. *Please, stop touching yourself.*

Stiller looked back and forth between the two of them. "Donkey Kong."

Ana put a hand to her forehead. "Oh. Yeah. Okay."

Logan had forgotten where they were. Kissing a woman in the middle of the governor's banquet was definitely on the get-your-ass-written-up-again list.

"You probably have cop stuff to do." Ana rubbed her lips.

"Yeah." He cleared his throat. "And you have Donkey Kong stuff to do."

Her face softened, and she smiled. "I'll see you around."

Clusters of men grumbled as he snaked through the crowd. The governor had promised to take every question, even if it took all night. *Fuck that.* Whatever was occupying the governor's time needed to scoot along to keep the inevitable speech on schedule.

The holdup stood beside Camden in a pair of tight-ass jeans and a creamy pink sweater, talking with her hands. Whatever she saw in Forrest, Logan wanted someone to see in him. His cousin was a divorced train wreck when he'd met her, fifteen years her senior, and now he had his shit together like he'd never lost it. And Forrest bent the rules for her. When he'd been married to Jessica, he'd lived by the book and never thought twice about it.

Camden poured Patience a hot chocolate and handed her a cookie. Logan's face burned at the attention he smothered her with. The asshole didn't care about her, the whales, the oil workers, the troopers, or the people of Alaska.

Money. It would always be his bottom line.

But there the motherfucker was—nodding, smiling, touching her arm at the perfect intervals. Like they were instructed, one of his clones whispered in Camden's ear to remind him to move on. He waved his assistant off.

Fire crept up Logan's neck. It was like a wolf closing

in on a bunny. Mitchell's arrest had to put a kink in the governor's plan. Would he recruit someone else or just handle Patience himself?

A tremor of panic forced him forward. He shoved a few doughnut holes in his mouth before breaking up the little chatfest.

"Governor, the crowd is getting antsy." He wiped powdered sugar off his lips.

Camden glared at him over Patience's head. "They can wait."

Patience downed her Styrofoam cup. "No. I'm sorry I've kept you so long."

Camden stuck his hand behind his back and an assistant placed a card in it. Logan cringed at their robotics. He moved, they moved. And if they moved first? They were jobless. Not one of them had a set of balls.

"If there's any time left in the day, come see me. I'd love to continue our conversation." Camden took a pen from his shirt pocket and wrote on the card. "Just swing by my room."

And to think Mrs. Camden didn't have anything to worry about with her husband in the Artic.

Patience's bright eyes darkened as she took the card. She flicked at it then clutched it in her fist. "Thanks."

She spun on a heel and left. Good girl.

"Thank you, Trooper Jones," Camden huffed.

"Not. A. Problem." He smiled.

Bob, or Bobby, or whatever the hell his name was, appeared from the assistant pool. "Governor Camden, the girl—Patience Cline—she's sleeping with Trooper Locke."

The little shit was getting tased the minute Logan got a chance. How the fuck did he know that?

They all stared at Logan. Camden smirked. The snitch smiled to himself like a puppy waiting for a pat on the head.

Logan straightened and brushed the doughnut crumbs off his uniform. "And?"

"Other than that he's on the job." Camden shrugged and rolled his sleeves down. "I bet the family is really proud."

One time. If Logan could pick one time to take his damn uniform off and plow his fist into someone's face, this would be it.

The family didn't recognize Logan and Forrest as Lockes anymore, but the feeling was mutual. They'd traded the name for money a long time ago. Forrest had refused to run the family's fleet of fishing vessels by his father's rules. Wouldn't take money from the employees to bribe the rule-makers, and he sure as hell wasn't going to sell illegally. Logan had never made it to the front office let alone to one of the ships. He'd partied out of college—spent his monthly allowance on alcohol until his parents dropped him off at rehab. Forrest was the only one waiting for him when he got out. The family's millions, and the blood that ran through their veins, meant nothing.

"As proud as your wife would be," he said.

Camden chuckled. "I might give my old football coach, your Uncle Joseph, a call. Let him know what good work his nephew and son are doing for me."

Forrest's father was a stern son of a bitch. He'd worked so hard in his life he thought he deserved it all.

Last Logan heard, the family had welcomed Forrest's ex-wife back with open arms.

They'd get endless amusement if they heard of the twenty-four-year-old North Carolina transplant. To an outsider, it might look like Forrest was just trying to prove he still had it going after a girl like Patience. But Logan knew better.

Fuck them. Fuck Camden.

"Be sure to tell Joe I said 'hi' and 'It's a shame the troopers seized one of his vessels last month.'" Logan had loved that morning wake up call.

Camden's arrogant smile slipped. "We need to have a little talk about Mitchell Wilson later. That's all for now, Trooper Jones."

Logan swallowed his dismissal and headed for the kitchen. Shit was going to get ugly.

He slid between two stainless steel doors, keeping an eye on the banquet through one of the windows. "Deadhorse 520 to Deadhorse 171. What's your twenty?"

"Out front. Wrapping up with Barrow PD."

"Ten-four."

The smell of fried food hit his nose, and he grabbed a handful of crispy calamari off the end of the food service line and stuffed them in his mouth. Forrest's father had a power Logan didn't understand, and Governor Camden's hold was wrapping around Logan just as tight. Mitchell had said he'd deny any involvement with Camden in court. Logan and Forrest couldn't go around accusing the governor of Alaska of conspiracy without solid evidence and expect to keep everything they ever worked for.

人

Forrest brushed flakes of ice off his shoulders and scanned the banquet crowd. A sea of bodies formed a crescent around Governor Camden. His voice rose above the murmurs as his speech commenced.

Forrest's pulse came to life as he searched for Patience.

"Your nine o'clock," said Logan's voice over the radio.

He spotted Stiller then shifted until he could see Patience. Tension had her face scrunched up. Whatever her blue-haired friend was telling her, she wasn't listening. She stared through him. To Paul and Ana talking behind them? To one of the few tourists caught in the whirlwind of the governor's campaign showing off their photographs of the Arctic sunrise?

Logan came up beside him with a plate of chips and dip and brownies.

"What happened?" Forrest eyed the food. "You don't ever eat that shit."

Logan dragged the back of his hand along his mouth. "Camden got a hold of Patience a few minutes ago."

Forrest glared at him. "And where were you?"

"Doing my job," Logan said. "I'm not the one fucking Miss North Carolina on a twenty-four-hour security detail. They know, by the way. Mitchell must have told Bobby."

Forrest ignored the heaviness settling on his chest. "Or they've been watching us the whole time too."

"What the fuck did we stumble into?" Logan muttered.

Whatever it was, Forrest wasn't backing down. "I started the paper trail. I noted in the arrest report

Mitchell's claims about the governor. Said he seemed under the influence, so, that should buy us some time before HQ takes any of this seriously."

Webs lay over Deadhorse, trapping the lies with the truth. Forrest had to leave some breadcrumbs behind to find his way back out.

Logan's phone started ringing and he dug it out of his pocket, glanced at it, then shoved it back in.

"Who was it?" Forrest asked.

"Nobody." He scooped a glob of dip on a single chip. "I'll check in with you in a bit."

Forrest stared after Logan. Nobody was somebody, but he'd have to figure that out later. He made a beeline for Patience, unable to move fast enough through the space between them.

"Forrest." She exhaled.

"Are you okay?"

She glanced at her teammates then patted his arm. "I'm fine. I was just telling them how the governor wants to talk to me more about our research. Me and Paul might go up to his room tonight."

Acid crept up his throat. "I don't know if that's a good idea."

She shrugged. "We might not get another chance like this. The marine institute called. We fly home tomorrow."

A bundle of feelings uncoiled from his chest, and he took a deep breath. "That's for the best."

Her smile never reached her sad eyes. "I know. It's just close. The data's so close."

Before he could stop himself, he cupped her cheek. "Today was *close*."

Other than their words and the beating of his heart, there was only silence around Forrest. Nothing burned as bright as she did. Strangers faded while she flickered with something he couldn't seem to get enough of.

11

Outlier

Patience eyed a pair of zebra-striped pajama pants that lay in a neat pile in her suitcase. They hid Logan's Glock. Deeper in her luggage lay a candle wrapped in her father's tie and stuffed inside a U.S. Marine Corp beanie. She'd tried to bring her family along for the journey. Imagining her father telling a client that his daughter conducted research in the Arctic Circle sent chills down her spine. Compared to her brother's travels, Deadhorse was a speck on the map, but he would understand how big it was in her world. Her mother's candle—a light Patience liked to think helped her mom see her through the clouds had come too.

There'd be other assignments. There'd be more whales. But this had been her first shot, and she'd failed.

Leaving Forrest behind was just the icing on this three-layer cake of bullshit.

She unwrapped the gun from her pants and

rewrapped it in a fuzzy teal sock and zipped it up in her makeup bag. It fit in an extra pocket within her laptop case without too much of a bulge. Weapon stashed, she went to Paul's room. All his maps and charts were packed away. An extra change of clothes hung over the desk chair.

"What do we have for the governor?" His dark eyes seemed more tired than usual.

"The works." Patience patted her laptop bag. "Threw some oil spill photos in the presentation."

He squinted at her. "Are you really going to wear that?"

"My 'Save the Whales' T-shirt?" She looked down at the sweating, hot pink beluga whale drinking a glass of lemonade. "Absolutely."

He chuckled as they walked into the hallway. "I'm going to have to get me one of those."

Maybe she'd get him one with a neon green whale. Maybe she'd get the whole team 'I'm sorry I fucked up the mission' T-shirts.

They rounded the corner, and Forrest and Logan jerked their heads around. Uneasiness drifted from their mirroring stances outside the governor's room. Forrest let them inside, hovering so close to Patience she worried the others would notice.

"I'll be right outside the door," he whispered.

Governor Camden rose from a table littered with coffee and sweet treats. "Paul. So nice of you to accompany Ms. Cline."

Paul's smile lines deepened. "Thought I'd take one last crack at you."

They shook hands like sworn enemies too old and

tired to care about the other's position. Patience tried to inch away from Forrest who'd crept from his post by the door and into the room. No one else noticed his death stare.

"Coffee, Paul?" Governor Camden looked up mid-pour.

"Sure. I'll take a glazed while I'm at it too."

The governor handed the cup over and winked at Patience. "My assistant is on his way up with some of that hot chocolate you like."

"Thanks." The gesture was a bit much, but she smiled anyway.

Camden sat and placed a napkin in his lap. "That'll be all Trooper Locke. Why don't you and Trooper Jones take the rest of the night off."

"Actually," Forrest said, leaning against the back of the empty chair between Patience and the governor. "I was hoping I could stick around. I used to read MMO surveys. It'd be interesting to hear from the people who collect and interpret the data."

Patience's mouth fell open. Warmth and pride filled her belly, even though his interest was probably only ever work-related.

"Since you don't let Patience do a lot of talking," Governor Camden said, motioning to the empty seat. "Join us. She has quite a lot to say."

Paul cocked his head to the side. Patience focused on a framed Arctic wolf photograph, leaning away from her boss's curious stare. What had Forrest done to piss off the governor? How did he even know about them?

Already the smallest person at the table, she cowered in the tension. Part of her felt like she would have been better off without Forrest there.

"Why don't I start?" Paul patted her shoulder, and she tried not to die inside.

"Sure." She forced a smile.

In and out of the conversation, focused and then in a haze, Patience tried to contribute to Paul's points in hopes that her relationship with Forrest wasn't pulling at their minds the same way it was hers. Facts made her stronger, though, her voice steadier as she presented them. Offshore drilling endangered hundreds of species, the environment, and Alaska's native tribes that inhabited the coasts. Massive, wondrous creatures that swam the oceans could disappear from the earth forever.

The governor folded his arms across his chest. "I'll have to share all of this information with your father, Forrest."

Patience's short-lived high from managing to get all of the information out without stumbling plummeted. What did Forrest's dad have to do with this?

Forrest shifted in his seat. "I'm not sure what this has to do with the fisheries."

"I don't know if my friend here has told you," Camden slapped Forrest on the back and looked between Patience and Paul, "but Locke Fishing Industries is funding my party's super PAC. The CEO has shown deep interest in offshore drilling, and as a beneficiary of his funds, I must entertain that interest."

Patience hit the back of her chair one vertebrae at a time. In a split second, everything changed. She'd embarked on a relationship with a man who had ties to the very thing she was trying to stop. Ties he'd so easily forgotten to mention. Is that why he was in Deadhorse? To keep an eye on his father's investment?

Paul brushed his pants off. "Must be nice having a trooper on the payroll."

Forrest's chair skidded back. "I don't know anything about this."

"You said you read the surveys, yourself." Paul stood, his chin level with Forrest's shoulders. "You had to when you were harvesting marine mammals' food source for human consumption."

"I haven't been a part of that business for ten years." Forrest's voice dissipated into a dull echo in Patience's ears.

The governor's eyes locked with hers. His tight, pinched face kept faltering and spreading into a smile. She wasn't even a pawn in this game, let alone a player. A larger, complex, and more corrupted world had scooped her dream up.

"It's just a coincidence you're here then?" Paul asked. "Unless you'd like a formal complaint made with your captain, I'd suggest you'd back up, Trooper Locke."

Forrest peered down at Patience from his stand-off with the older man. There was plenty for him to explain, maybe too much to get through the red tape, but it couldn't happen here. Not when everything pointed back at the man she trusted.

"As you can see," Governor Camden said, holding out his palms. "My hands are tied. I appreciate everything the Marine Mammal Institute does for the state of Alaska and I encourage you to keep doing it."

Patience flicked the auto-pilot switch on and hastily packed up their presentation materials. "Enjoy the rest of your time in Deadhorse, Governor."

"Stay away from my MMO, you hear me?" Paul's words bounced off the walls behind Patience as she rushed into the hallway.

Logan held his hands out to slow her down. She dug the teal sock out of her bag and forced it into his hand.

"Whoa, Pay. What happened?" He looked over her head into the room.

"Like you don't know." She held her breath, begging the emotion in her voice to cease. "Tell him...tell Forrest...just tell him I said bye."

"What the fuck?" he whispered.

She took off down the hallway, her bag swinging around her hips. Coincidences discredited everything in research. A misleading correlation the mind couldn't un-see, un-feel. Fate, the universe—none of it had brought her and Forrest together.

Forrest could vomit at the governor's shit-eating grin.

"Come on in, Logan, and take a seat." Governor Camden waved Forrest's cousin inside.

Forrest returned Logan's worried stare; his feet planted to the floor to keep from running after Patience. They were in Deadhorse for a reason. Pawned off by a family they'd been estranged from for years.

"Take a seat, boys," Camden said. "We're all in this together now."

"What's going on?" Logan took Patience's empty chair.

The governor pointed his steepled fingers to Forrest's seat.

He pushed the chair under the table. They couldn't be pulled into this. They'd worked too hard for the lives they had now.

The governor chuckled. "Relax, son. Things are going to get a little sticky in Deadhorse, and I just want to make sure we're all on the same page."

Forrest leaned against the table and leveled his eyes with Logan's, trying to convey how serious their situation had become. "Locke industries is interested in offshore drilling. They're funding the campaign. That's why we're here."

Logan's face turned blood red. "Sons-a-bitches."

"Listen, here." Governor Camden shifted to the edge of his seat. "I want to thank you for getting Mitchell Wilson out of here. I can't have disgruntled voters smearing my name like that. Forrest, I really appreciate the discretion you used in that arresting report. I would never condone such a thing, and I think you know that."

Forrest slammed his palm against the table. "He broke into a woman's room with a nine-millimeter. Said you sent him there to gain access to her research."

Camden cracked his neck and folded his hands in his lap. "You don't really believe that, do you?"

"It's not about what I believe." Forrest stared into the governor's unwavering eyes. "It's about what I can prove."

"All we know is that Mr. Wilson had it out for the researchers." Crease lines deepened around Camden's eyes. "And thank God you were in Ms. Cline's room to intercept him. Who knows what he would have done to her otherwise."

His presence in Patience's room was another thing

he'd been vague about in the report. Irresponsible, inappropriate, and reckless behavior never followed Forrest's name. But it would if someone brought light to his relationship with Patience. Logan had already called him out on it, warned him of the consequences, and here he stood, proud of one thing—he had gotten her out of Deadhorse

"You know what happens to people like Mitchell?" Logan said, leaning back and interlacing his fingers behind his head. "They get caught."

"That's why I chose you two." Camden rubbed his chin. "You won't get caught."

"No one will, because this is over," Forrest reminded the governor. "The MMO team is out of here. I think it's best if you get back to your campaign."

Forrest could deal with his family and the governor. Nothing about their pairing scared him. With Patience out of the mix, he should be able to get him and Logan out of this mess in one piece.

"Actually," Governor Camden said as he smoothed his hair back. "I put a call in to the marine institute when I caught wind they were leaving. I just didn't think it was fair."

Forrest leaned against the back of a chair and it creaked under his weight. Fury and fear swallowed him.

"I offered one of my troopers to stay with the researchers for the remainder of the survey." The governor nodded, smiling to himself, and then squinted up at Forrest. "They'll get back to us in the morning, but I think it's safe to say you can start packing. Maria has a room for you closer to the team."

"Do you think this is a game?" Logan shot to his feet.

Forrest grabbed Logan's shoulder, tremors seeping into his hand as he held him in place. If the governor wanted to keep Forrest off his tracks, fine. The distance wouldn't stop him from collecting evidence. But there was one thing the governor had to understand, and Forrest would be damned if the man didn't know it already.

"You're not going to use me to get to that research. If someone gave you the impression that I was your guy, well, they're next on my list." Forrest wouldn't stop at Camden; he'd go after Locke Industries, too. "Are we clear?"

Governor Camden stood, chuckling as he rolled his sleeves down. "You like that badge on your chest, Trooper Locke?"

The shiny brass had gotten heavier, but no matter how much it weighed on him, he'd always stand behind it. "As much as you like your freedom."

"We'll see about that." The governor slid his hands into his pockets. "Thank you for your service, Forrest."

∧

Logan paced, counting his wide steps. "He's separating us. Making it harder to watch him."

Forrest shoved a stack of white T-shirts into a navy-blue duffel bag. "Just do your job and keep your eyes open."

They should have known what they were walking into. Family members patrolling together should have been a red flag. Forrest was an easy pick for campaign security detail. He was a trooper the force was proud of. A trooper who could use a little time away from home. Logan, on the other hand, lived on the verge of disciplinary suspension. Always.

"I'm not going to make it out of this one," Logan muttered.

Forrest zipped his bag up and threw it over his shoulder. "What are you talking about? We're going to be fine."

"You're going to be fine," he corrected him. "Camden's going to have my badge before I even make it back to Fairbanks."

"Like hell he is." Forrest pointed at him. "I don't care what he tries to do, the truth is coming out."

"He's setting us up." Logan sat on the edge of the bed and caught his head in his hands. "We have a motive to help him, to harass and threaten the researchers just like Mitchell did."

"Says who?" Forrest asked. "You really think he'll get five people to go along with that story?"

Logan tried to suppress the itch that haunted him. Escape wasn't possible. Oblivion wasn't achievable.

Live it. Feel it. Deal with it.

He'd come to master high-stress situations in his own way. He'd kept his head clear plenty of times before. All he had to do was believe that he could reach the level of serenity he needed. *Breathe.*

The vibrating on his hip tore down the person he built up every morning.

"*God damn it,*" No matter how hard Logan squeezed his head, he couldn't stop shaking. "He's been calling every fifteen minutes since the banquet."

Forrest took the phone out of Logan's holster. "Jesus Christ."

The present? The future? Bring it on. But his past? It had a way of latching onto Logan, relentlessly reminding him how it could weave into his life whenever it wanted to. Joseph Locke wasn't calling his son because he knew he couldn't break him down. He called his nephew, the one who might not be able to say no.

"Look at me. On your feet." Forrest pulled him to his feet, forcing him to make eye contact, and put a hand on each shoulder. "My dad's not going to bully you into anything. You're not going to let him do that to you. You're not going to let anyone do that to you."

Emotion burned in Logan's throat. "Sorry. I'm just... fucking struggling."

His cousin was the stronger, better man. A version of himself Logan would never become.

Forrest grabbed him and crushed him to his chest. "I wouldn't have anyone else by my side, you know that, right?"

Logan's lungs relaxed and he caught his breath. "Yeah."

"Good." Forrest patted his back with both hands and pulled back. "Don't talk to him. I'll deal with it."

Logan tried to swallow the residual panic assaulting the roof of his mouth. "Okay."

"It'll pass." Forrest half-smiled.

Logan closed his eyes and his tense shoulders fell. "It always does."

How many times had they repeated that mantra? It always worked, but it may not get him through letting Forrest down. Logan knew it was just a matter of time before he failed him.

"Make sure you check your new room out." He wiped

his nose. "Cameras, mics."

"I will. You're going to be fine. I'll check in with you in the morning. Okay?"

"Yeah. Okay."

⋏

Logan hit one hundred push-ups and kept going. Exhaustion would be the only way he slept tonight. Sweat dripped off his nose and onto the phone lying on the ground underneath him. The calls had bumped up to every ten minutes. Joseph didn't even try calling from a different number, just the same one, over and over. He knew Logan couldn't turn the phone off and had to be available at all times. Forrest had said he'd handle it, but why hadn't he already?

The burning in his arms and back began to fade as he pumped harder against the ground. Cooling sweat made the hairs rise all over his body. The phone glowed and shivered, and he collapsed.

Fuck it. You can handle this. You can do this.

He answered and rolled onto his back. "Stop terrorizing me."

"Logan," Joseph sighed.

"Stop calling," he said. "We're well past harassment."

"How are you?" Joseph asked. His uncle had always spoken to him like he was a valued member of the family. It only made the warm, genuine feeling he exuded that much more awful.

The muscles in Logan's face twitched. When his father had passed away, Uncle Joe had filled his shoes. He'd always wanted to make the man proud but never knew how. Sam had been incapable of living up to Joe's expectations, and Forrest had never wanted to.

"Tired," he answered. "Thankfully, there's nothing for us to talk about. Have a good—"

"Your father would have never pegged you for a state trooper." He laughed. "You know that?"

"Probably not." The troopers had brought him home a lot has a kid.

"Your mother's really proud of you. It seems like every Sunday dinner she's got a different news article on you."

Logan spoke with his mother around the holidays. She even came to Fairbanks once or twice a year to visit him in her diamonds and furs.

"I don't know what you're up to, Uncle Joe," he said, "but I don't want anything to do with it."

"I know you've got your mind made up about me," Joseph cleared his throat, "and I know your cousin has shaped your opinions, but I want you to know that I'm impressed with your career in law enforcement, and your sobriety."

Logan refused to soak in the words. *Too little, too late.* "You didn't call to tell me that."

"I've waited a long time to make this call, son."

Logan couldn't fill the silence. Sweat and tears mixed in his eyes.

"Are you ready to come home?"

Logan shook his head, but he couldn't answer. The temptation of getting back the life he lost was too great. No more long days and nights. No more snow and darkness. No more checks and balances. No more violence and crime.

"I can't," he managed to whisper.

"We all have a price."

And you know I'm a cheap, broken bastard.

Logan stared at his uniform in a heap on the floor. His vest hung on the back of a chair, and his sidearm lay on its side on top of the desk, pointing at him.

"What do you want?" he asked.

12

Blurry

Forrest dropped his bags in Mitchell's old room. The made bed, fresh towels, and unopened toiletries strummed a once unmovable chord. Suspects rolled off Forrest like water, but this was different. This time, the scope was beyond one assailant, one shot-caller. His family had cast a net and hadn't just tangled him and Logan inside, but Patience too.

Dim yellow lights lit the hallway as he rushed out his door and into Paul's room. He could only hope the marine institute had denied the governor's offer and ordered them home. The pit of Forrest's stomach ate up that hope when Paul answered the door with a phone to his ear. He instructed Forrest to sit, but he couldn't be idle when his brain sped forward like a steam engine.

"Will do." Paul stared at the phone before dropping it.

"Your director?" Forrest asked.

Paul spun around in a daze then plopped down on his neatly made bed. "That was Corey Anderson, the MMO Patience replaced."

Knots bound up Forrest's stomach.

A thin sheen of sweat glistened on Paul's face. "The entire survey has been compromised."

"What did he tell you?"

"He didn't break his legs in a snowmobile accident." Paul's shoulders fell. "Someone took a bat to him."

The need to gather more information, and the desperation to see Patience alive and safe tore Forrest in half. "Tell me everything he said. Now."

Paul rested his hand over his mouth and stared at the wall. "It was Mitchell. During his rotations home from the rig, he was tracking down MMOs."

Sweat sealed Forrest's shirt to his back. Mitchell could have easily intimidated and coerced Patience if Forrest hadn't been in the right place at the right time.

"Corey backed out," Paul continued. "He tried to give the money back, but—"

"There's no backing out." Forrest knew that.

"Is that why you're here?" Paul adjusted his glasses. "To make sure the job gets done?"

"There's only one job I have here," Forrest said, pointing at the other man. "And don't think for a second it's anything other than upholding the law."

Paul looked away, his face solemn. "Everyone has a price."

"Only they can decide what it is." Forrest moved so he could be in front of Paul's gaze and stared down at him. "Call the institute. Now. Get your team out of here."

Because I have a price, and she's four doors down.

A weak smile rose beneath his eyes. "I already did. I was instructed to accept the governor's offer. If the survey isn't complete, it'll be another year of exploratory drilling in the Beaufort."

That's why the governor needed them to stay. There was no money in exploration. Camden had dug his claws in deep—deeper than Forrest had thought. "It's not safe here. Please."

Paul shrugged. "There's nothing I can do about it. I'll comply with whatever the governor needs to get my team home safe. The survey is meaningless now as it is."

Once Forrest had uncovered the family business' corruption, he'd left. A decade later, and it had followed him all the way to the Arctic. The oil industry had been his idea way back when. A next-level investment with high risks and high rewards. Maybe the fish had finally capped out. If he knew his father, every resource had been used to swing the research. Hundreds of thousands in pay off money—spent.

"Just keep doing what you're doing." Forrest bottled the need to check on Patience, physically see her and touch her. "Don't interact with the governor or his team. Do you understand?"

Paul shifted. "What about Trooper Jones?"

Uneasiness came over Forrest, but he pushed it away. "My cousin will do whatever he can to help us."

He refused to believe Logan would throw his life away for Locke Industries.

"Okay," Paul said, nodding.

"You'll get me if anyone contacts you?"

"Yes."

Forrest swung the door open and stomped out. He

stalked down the hallway, boots loud on the ground. It killed him to knock at Patience's room. Every passing millisecond stung. Every absent breath burned. Sirens blared between his ears.

Open the door.

Patience answered, hair pushed back with a white headband and wearing a black, oversized long-sleeve T-shirt. Large teal letters crossed her chest.

Fresh-faced and angry, she glared at him, the blue of her eyes becoming storm cloud gray.

He breathed. "You're all right."

A hand shot to her hip. "What do you want?"

"I just needed to see you."

Anger and fear stopped fighting one another, and his pulse slowed. Explaining himself, explaining his family—none of it matter as long as she was safe.

Her face softened, and her arm fell to her side. "I've got a lot of packing to do."

"About that..." He pulled his cap off and shoved it in his back pocket. "The governor called the institute and offered a trooper to keep your team safe."

She crossed her arms then ran her fingers across her lips, eyes focused down the hallway. A chuckle and smile formed beneath her hand, and she shook her head. "Paul's not going to buy that." She shoved past him. "And neither am I."

"Patience. Wait." Forrest reached for her as she ran.

She stopped at Paul's door and knocked with rapid fire, foot tapping the ground as fast as her knuckles rapped against the wood. Forrest retreated to his new room when she disappeared inside. She would be livid, upset about the research, but she needed to hear it for herself. Things in Deadhorse were not what they appeared to be.

⋏

Patience floated back into the hallway and wandered to her room. Every moment of her education and career had led up to this place. The combination of offshore drilling and over-fishing had sped up the inevitable for her beloved whales. Now, none of it mattered. The data, the researchers—all mapped out ahead of time. A show she'd stumbled into without knowing there was a part to play.

If it wasn't thirteen below outside, she might haul ass after the sunset, but if the cold didn't get her, a starving polar bear would.

Forrest stood in the doorway of Mitchell's old room, shoulder leaning against the frame and eyes laser-focused on her. Pieces of his combed-back hair had forgotten their place in his meticulous image and fallen onto his forehead.

She tried to look away, keep a death-grip on her ever-growing fury and convince herself that exceptions were for fools, and she was done being one of those. She couldn't help how everything around him blurred, her brain seeking the space he occupied, the air he breathed, the invisible force he carried around with him.

She loved that damn uniform.

"I hate that uniform," she muttered.

"What?" He straightened, and his hands settled on his hips.

She squeezed her eyes shut, scared Mitchell would appear from behind Forrest even though he was in a jail cell in Barrow. "I guess there weren't any more rooms available?"

He didn't answer. Quiet shuffling came from across the hall. She peeled one eye open as royal blue slid off his shoulders and down his arms.

Concentrate.

The belt, gun, and cuffs went next.

The short sleeve of his white T-shirt slid up his bicep as he put a hand to his chest. "I want to talk to you. Not the trooper. Just me."

"That's impossible." She stared at the ground.

"It's not."

"You really think there's a difference between the man and the cop?" A sexy uniform, a wearable trophy for a badge, and the power of the law didn't turn Forrest off and turn the trooper on.

"There better be."

The determination in his voice flooded her. If she could keep her eyes trained on the dark stain on the floor, she might be able to say what she needed to. "Your family bought a politician. It's legal, but it's not right. And you—"

"They don't just buy politicians." He bit his bottom lip and stepped into the hallway. "They buy inspectors, regulators, bankers. People like Mitchell. People like you."

Patience tried to swallow the ball in her throat. "Corey. The others..."

Had they been weak? Scared? If it wasn't for Forrest, would she be down that same road?

Forrest came closer, close enough to touch. "Whether people want to be bought or not, they'll do whatever is necessary to get what they want."

Patience stepped back into her room on a wobbly foot. "What about people like you?"

"Troopers?" He nodded. "Sometimes. But not me. Never me. I'll never do their bidding again."

Behind the anger in his glowing green eyes, beneath every tense muscle fighting his skin and on the tail end of every word, desperation slipped through. Every step he took forward, she took one back. He closed her door behind him with a gentle push.

"The governor sent Mitchell after you." His lips twisted to the side. "I should have told you."

Nausea swirled down into the pit of Patience's stomach. The edge of the bed hit the backs of her knees. "Why didn't you tell me?"

Forrest knelt in front of her, stopping short of grasping her hand. "I couldn't make accusations against the governor without evidence."

Patience sat and waved a hand to dispel the panic so she could think. The stakes had been high since the beginning. Team October was the final stretch of a five-month-long survey to determine if whale populations were stable enough to allow for offshore drilling. The governor and Locke Industries had almost sealed the deal.

She never imagined she'd be in this kind of crossfire. Always too blind. Too naive to see what was really happening. Although in the midst of a freefall, she wasn't quite ready to hit the ground.

"I don't need evidence." She pointed to herself. "You should have told me. I'm my first line of defense. Not you or anybody else."

Disappointment settled heavy in her chest, more than anything else. All along she'd thought he'd been embracing her, believing things no one had ever tried to believe in her before.

"You're right and I'm sorry." His head swayed side to side, his eyes never leaving hers. "I thought the less you knew, the better."

He didn't have faith in her. *Breathe, Pay. It's okay.*

"I didn't even stand a chance out here." She raised her arms at her half-packed room. "The whales don't even stand a chance."

Forrest placed a gentle hand on her leg. "This isn't over yet."

She pulled in a deep breath as his fingers glided up her shin and around her calf. "I know," she said. "I'm supposed to just keep doing what I'm doing. Pretending. Paul said he'll deal with the governor, so I don't have to."

Sobs tried to take over her body, but she wouldn't let them. Paul needed her to stay level. The team needed her.

"Listen," Forrest swallowed. "I know it looks bad me being here—"

"Fucking awful is how it looks." She ripped her headband off and wrapped it around her fist. "It's like Camden planted you here to make sure we do what we're told."

Why did he insist on playing with the truth? There was no salvaging their relationship, no excuse that could fix this. He made his choices, and she had to make hers.

"That's not true, Patience." Forrest placed both hands firmly on her knees. "Please listen to me."

"Just admit it." She pushed his hands away and ran

to her luggage. She knelt down and tried to unzip the damn thing, but it wouldn't budge. "You knew all about this."

If he dragged it out any longer, it was going to break her. There'd be more opportunities to help the whales, but there was only one Forrest, and this was the end of what they had.

"I need to tell you something." His clear, heavy voice sliced through the room.

Patience stood and turned around, her heart dragging her closer and closer to a cliff.

"It's something I don't have to tell most people, they just know." With his jaw set tight, he stood tall and pinned her in place with his gaze. "I'll die for my job."

Chills raised the hairs on her forearms. She'd known that about Forrest since the moment she met him, but here she was, assigning their relationship the inevitability everything in the world had and forcing it on him. Placing blame and running.

"I don't know what else to tell you," he said. "There are a million things I could say, but I'm scared to death I'll say the wrong thing."

The way his eyes glistened before casting down stole her breath, robbed her of whatever control she had.

"I will say," He reached for the door, drawing her toward him how the moon pulls the tide, "that I'll be by your side until November. Paul...Ana...Stiller...Them too. And after this is all over, the governor is going to answer for it."

He nodded at her breathy silence, and she didn't stop him when he opened the door and closed it behind him.

Every nerve in Patience's body settled. She wasn't

just fighting Forrest, but herself too. Putting him through a test didn't fix her insecurities. There was no victory in him saying the right words, even if he didn't realize he had.

13

Undercover

Ana Smith zipped up her flight suit then pulled her long dark hair into a ponytail. After six years in the Air Force flying F-15s and then two as an instructor, she'd left to try the whole family thing but didn't get further than a fiancé. Puttering around a cookie-cutter house in despicable Good Housekeeping fashion wasn't for her, and neither was matrimonial prison. So, she became a one-woman charter for her home state of Alaska.

Being a small business owner proved challenging enough most days, but she missed the adrenaline and the thrill of the military. Then the FBI called.

She passed through the bathroom her and Patience's room shared, nudging the young woman's things from the edge of the counter to a safe, neat place. Ana didn't do roommates. She didn't really have a lot of friends. No reason to bother with people who wouldn't be around. Why she'd taken to Patience, though, she didn't know.

The more intelligence she gathered, the more she wished she'd had a wild little sister growing up.

"Pay," Ana said, stepping into the room, the contents of a makeup bag skidding across the floor.

Patience crouched beneath a desk littered with stickers and thumbtacks. "I'm going to die if I can't find my Chapstick."

A swollen, half-zippered piece of luggage lay on its side, electrical cords hung in a tangle off the edge of the desk, and a map of the artic dangled from one corner on the wall.

"I love what you've done with the place." Ana itched to straighten the disarray. Order. She needed order.

Patience stood, one hand rubbing on Chapstick like a madwoman and the other planted on her hip. "I'm going to call it," She said, spinning around, "Zero Fucks by Pay. Yep. Zero Fucks."

"Uh-huh." Ana took a tentative step toward Patience, reached for her friend's disheveled hair but pulled back. "Were you up all night?"

Patience let her shiny lips go with a pop. "Yep."

Girl talk was never Ana's thing. She gave shit for advice, but she wasn't just there for a paycheck. Opportunity awaited. "Maybe you could braid my hair before we go down for breakfast?"

The flood gates would open with Patience distracted. Thanks to the governor, Ana had a couple more weeks to uncover what was really happening in Deadhorse. If she had to wade through silly insecurities, pangs of homesickness, and evil ex-boyfriends, she would.

The frantic look in Patience's eyes brightened. "French braid?"

Ana's objective was to identify threats to Team October's research. She'd reported Mitchell Wilson's first move to the FBI, then his second attempt which Forrest thwarted. The troopers' presence had surprised her but had been a welcome sight on her first assignment. If another attempt was made, she needed to be ahead of it.

"Whatever you want," she said.

Patience spun the desk chair around. "I thought you'd never ask."

Coffee hit Ana's nose and she walked faster, leaving behind Patience and Forrest's awkward conversation and Stiller's morning blues outside the cafeteria. She dipped into the lobby bathroom, assessed the rope of hair down her back, and then left for the hotel exit. A rainbow of light wrapped around the horizon in every direction as she dug her phone out of her pocket. The crisp air sharpened her breaths.

"We have developments in Deadhorse," she said.

FBI Agent Grace Martinez cleared her throat. Loud pops sounded in the background. "Hurry. I'm in the middle of something."

Ana relayed her tell-all conversation with Patience as gold seeped into the blue sky. Who knew what a little hair therapy could unveil?

"Forrest Locke is claiming ignorance," Grace mused. "Where is the other trooper on this? Trooper Jones?"

"Unclear at this time. They have a strong bond. I would be surprised to see them misaligned."

"Let's not assume any more about the troopers. What they do, not what they say, is going to make the difference." She puffed into the phone.

"Are you running?" Ana asked.

"I'm in pursuit. Increase contact and mic Patience's room. I want an update in eighteen hours."

"Yes, ma'am," Ana said.

She put her game face on and hurried back to the cafeteria.

Trooper Jones stood at the coffee station, swirling a wooden stirrer in his Yeti thermos. She'd nearly kissed this person of interest at the governor's banquet. From the first time she'd laid eyes on him, she'd been fighting an internal war with herself. Too close, and she might do more than the job she signed on to do. Too far, and she might accomplish nothing.

"Morning." She reached across him for a disposable cup.

He shifted silently, arrogant posture and cocky grin missing.

"I forgot they don't teach you manners at the academy." She ripped open two packets of sugar with her teeth.

"Fu—" His eyes met hers. "Morning."

"That's better." Ana breathed in the steamy brew warming her hands.

He turned away, voice raw and scratchy, "I'm surprised you have anything to say to me. I know your team's not happy."

Ana followed his worried gaze, wondering if a sleepless night had stolen his smooth, heavy tone, or if it was last night's revelation. "Why? Because of Forrest? I have to recalculate weights for the plane, edit evac protocols, run through drills with him. He's probably a much better student than you so..."

She elbowed his side, heat surging to her cheeks. *Why am I doing this? He could be a crooked cop.* At Quantico, they'd covered tactics on gathering information and how to perform minor surveillance. Not flirting. However, the more he revealed, the better off she'd be.

"I'm more of the teaching type." A faint smile pulled at his lips.

"I'd bet you have a lot left to learn."

More appealing than his dark hair in need of a cut, his heart-jolting smile and good boy trying to put on a bad boy attitude was his time stamp. Men like Logan didn't call. They didn't want anything more.

"I'm willing to find out." His tired words came to life, waking her more than any amount of caffeine could.

Even his cologne, like an oaky apple pie with just enough musk to remind her it was a man and not something she should eat with ice cream, found its way through her body.

"We can all dream." She stepped away—convinced lovey-dovey Patience had her slipping.

"Maybe I can see you tonight. If that's all right with the rest of them." He motioned toward the full table.

He worried what they all thought, and she had to find out if there was truly a reason to worry.

"That'll be up to me, Trooper Jones."

He smiled briefly and then pressed, "They're not pissed?"

"About what?" She wanted him to say it, to reveal the truth she already knew. "They should be happy they get to stay."

Logan frowned, deep lines cutting between his

eyebrows. "I'll be ready for class around nine tonight."

She quelled the butterflies in her stomach. "Bring paper and a pencil. You're going to want to take notes."

She cursed her need to have the last word. What was he going to think when he found out she was all talk?

He grinned, and his face turned bright pink. "May I be excused? I have a lot of work to do."

She stepped aside as the governor's entourage passed, wiping the sweat from her forehead. "Dismissed."

Forrest stood at his post in the airport hangar as Patience's team filed into the locker room to ready for another flight over the Beaufort. Ana offered a curt smile. Stiller judged him from head to toe. Patience tripped over her own feet.

Paul came from the Twin Otter plane with a black duffle bag. "This is Corey's gear. It may be a little short, but it should fit all right."

"You still want me to go up with you?" he asked.

Paul adjusted his Mariners cap and glanced at the closed locker room door. "I'm going to keep you close. Just to be safe."

Paul wanted to keep Locke Industries' role in the governor's campaign a secret and Forrest didn't see a reason to unsettle the rest of the team, but the fear in Paul's eyes unnerved him.

"I arrested the last man that tried to hurt your team," he said. "I'll do it again if I have to."

"I know. I'm thankful for that." Paul pushed his glasses up his nose and patted Forrest on the shoulder. "Suit up."

Forrest stepped into the locker room and all chatter stopped. Patience came from the women's bathroom between two walls of beige metal lockers, freezing mid-step in a gray and blue wet suit. It fit her like a second skin, sealing in the swells of her curves from her neck to her ankles. Fire scorched across Forrest's face and down his neck.

Stiller emerged behind her in the same color suit. "Thanks, Pay."

"Lay off the doughnuts, would you." She darted over to Ana.

Stiller's white smile flashed across the room. "You know I got to have that sugar."

Forrest dragged his stare away from Patience to Stiller. There was another man that could have helped him with his suit. Sure, teammates went out of their way to help each other, but this one was a man Patience's age. A man who was an outsider just like her. There was probably all kinds of interesting shit they had in common.

Get it together.

Forrest ran a hand down his face, took a deep breath, and the sweat on the back of his neck began to cool.

Stiller shuffled over to make room for him at the bench in front of the men's lockers. Paul threw his suit over his shoulder and disappeared into the men's room.

Forrest took the wet suit out of the bag and held it up. It would take all his might to get into it. The locker room was empty by the time he got the material up his thick thighs. He couldn't keep his thoughts from drifting into the past as he tried to force the suit up his body. Gear like this had saved his life a long time ago. The cradle of the sea had rocked too hard and he'd fallen overboard. It hadn't kept him from the vessel for long, though. His crew had needed him. The family business had needed him.

"Forrest?"

Bobby pins kept back the short pieces of Patience's hair, and a tiny ponytail stuck out the top of her head. The bulky suit swallowed her like an astronaut destined for things much greater than this place.

"Need some help?" she asked.

He looked down at his heaving, bare chest and the orange outer suit waiting on the bench. "Yeah."

She went to her locker and came back with a small, hot pink towel. "It helps if you're not sweaty."

Patience wiped the water-wicking fabric across his chest. The determination on her face eased with every pass—from his shoulders, down his arms to his ribs. He couldn't stop himself from smiling so he stared up at the ceiling. Having her take care of him created a strange and warm feeling. She hadn't thought twice about it.

A slow, wandering hand dragged the towel to his back. It melted the near-constant tension in his body, and he breathed deep and easy.

"We're going to make it through this," she whispered. *We're.*

Forrest tried to force words out, anything to reflect what it meant to him to be a couple. A unit. A team. Last night, he'd wondered if he'd done enough, wondered what it would take to keep her in his life. The peace she brought him had revived parts of himself he'd buried a long time ago.

He turned into her, tucked back the strands of hair

slipping free from the bobby pins, and kissed her cheek. "I know."

She blushed and tugged on his suit. "Let's wrestle you into this. I have work to do."

The ocean flowed in the opposite direction, creating a false sense of speed as they glided at ninety knots. Forrest wished this could be Patience's special place again. The bubble observation window in the Twin Otter plane held her image, and the pink horizon hid the sadness in her eyes. He'd get it all back for her. Dreams happened, and even in the throes of a nightmare, they could come true.

The oil rigs, like giant middle fingers sticking out of the tundra, drifted away in the distance. Frustration faded from Patience's voice with every animal sighting, and the keys on her laptop clicked easier and quieter. The data may be all for nothing, but the experience wasn't. Seeing her in her element only made his pride grow. This person, this scientist, had a command she wasn't aware of, and he loved it.

⋏

Back at The Aurora Hotel, Forrest went to his room while the team readied for dinner and sought the source of all their problems. He took his phone out of his pocket, scrolling for a distant contact. His father couldn't hide in the background for much longer.

"Trooper Locke? Is that you?" Joseph Locke laughed, and Forrest cringed. On too many occasions he'd been told they shared the same deep laughter.

"Just wanted to let you know I have a restraining order with your name on it." Forrest would follow through on the threat if Logan needed him to. There were only so many phone calls Logan could ignore before he finally answered.

"Take it easy." He chuckled. "I gave up on calling your cousin. Seems he's taken on some of your resolve."

"Don't call him again." Forrest started a slow pace from the furnace to the bathroom. "I'm serious."

"I just wanted to see if the governor was doing right by my money and not fucking around up there." Joseph yawned. "You know, I hear you have a girlfriend now. What's her name?"

Forrest flicked the safety on his firearm off then on. "What are you doing getting involved with the governor?"

"I'm all in, son. I need a big return on this investment or that's it."

Forrest closed his eyes. "You ran the company into the ground."

"You always said I would." He grew quieter. "Now if we can just get into the oil—"

"No, Dad." Forrest rubbed his eyes. "Do you have any idea what Camden is doing up here?"

"All I know is he gets the job done."

"He's threatening people. Since June, researchers have been harassed and intimidated." Forrest glared at the ceiling and bit his bottom lip. "That's what your money is paying for."

"This is nothing new to us, Forrest."

"It's wrong."

"You were always good at fixing problems. Why don't you come on back?"

"You can't fix this."

"You *can*." Joseph's earnestness bled through the

phone. "Come back. Be the CEO. We'll do it all on your terms."

"There's nothing to come back to." And there never would be.

"Everyone wants something, Forrest."

"There's nothing you can give me."

"I guess I'll just have Patience give me what I want."

"You—" Forrest chucked the phone as the line went dead. "Motherfucker."

Forrest couldn't let them get to Patience. If he had to open an investigation into the governor, then fine. If he had to open one into his father, he was ready. Forrest didn't play games. He wouldn't be a pawn, and neither would Patience.

$$\curlywedge$$

Patience flipped her towel-dried hair over in the bathroom and answered her ringing phone. The beating in her chest quickened. It was Corey.

"Hello?"

"Hey, Patience. This is Corey. You got a minute?"

Did she have a minute to understand why he sold out to the governor? Fuck yeah. "Sure. What's up?"

After two muffled voices made an exchange, a feminine throat cleared. "Patience, this is Agent Grace Martinez with the FBI."

"Corey, what is this?" She reached back until her fingertips touched the edge of the tub and sat down.

"I need to ask you some questions." Agent Martinez's level tone came across clear and crisp. "Corey told me what's going on in Deadhorse. This is about your safety."

"Um, okay."

Her flight instinct kicked in, like the force of hummingbird wings against the air, but there was nowhere to fly to. Panic strummed her heart, thumping the muscle against her chest wall.

"Has Governor Camden threatened you?" Agent Martinez asked.

Patience fanned her face with a shaky hand. "No, not directly."

"Have any of his aides or assistants threatened you?"

"No one but Mitchell." Anger and fear shook her words out.

"I've seen the arresting report, Patience. Trooper Locke's interpretation of Mr. Wilson's claims is brief and dismissive, but present. Mr. Wilson suffered extensive injuries from that arrest. Are you aware of that?"

"No." Nausea settled in Patience's empty stomach. Getting Forrest into trouble hadn't been her goal.

"Do you know why Mitchell broke into your room?"

"He told Trooper Locke the governor put him up to it, to gain access to my research."

Agent Martinez's tone lowered. "And then Trooper Locke contacted the marine institute?"

"That's right."

"Why was Trooped Locke in your room that morning?"

Uneasiness spilled down Patience's body. "To talk about the fight between Mitchell and Stiller."

"Do you feel safe around Trooper Locke?"

"Yes," she snapped. "Why?"

"And Trooper Jones?"

"Yes. Why are you asking me about the troopers?"

"Take a breath," she said. "I'm covering all of my

bases here. The FBI cannot move forward with an investigation until we can confidently connect Mr. Wilson to Governor Camden, or until the governor threatens you, your team, or the research directly. Do you understand?"

"Yes." She exhaled.

"We want to stop the harassment, intimidation, and coercion of researchers in Alaska."

"Good." Patience swallowed. "I'm sorry. This is a little overwhelming."

"We need your help."

Patience wiped away the clammy sweat crawling down her neck.

"Without you," Agent Martinez said, "endangered species have no voice. We need to stop this. Now."

"O-okay." Patience stammered. "What do you need me to do?"

"We've been fortunate to have Corey's help." Agent Martinez's gratefulness seeped through the line. "We would like yours as well but let me tell you what we have to do."

"I'm listening." Patience reached for phantom, long blonde locks to pull over her shoulder.

"We have to register you as a confidential informant."

Water stopped dripping from the showerhead, the last cloud of fog dissipated from the mirror, and the tiles beneath Patience's feet turned ice cold.

"It's for your protection," Agent Martinez explained. "If you're going to provide information to the FBI, I want to have resources ready to help you, to support you during this investigation, and to support you during a trial if it comes to that."

"I'm not sure about this." Patience squeezed her eyes shut, searching for answers in the dark. "The troopers can help, can't they?"

"The troopers cannot know about this. It's for your safety and theirs."

She had to protect Forrest. "Okay."

"Your time in Deadhorse can mean something. From what Corey has told me, it's doing more harm than good."

"I want to help. I really do."

"Patience, if a hefty sum of money appears in your bank account, and you're accused of accepting a bribe for the alteration of scientific data, *we* can help *you*."

"That won't happen." Patience wouldn't let it. "I don't even need the money."

Agent Martinez sighed, empathy lacing her words. "It already has."

No.

Patience opened the banking app on her phone and logged in. A ten-thousand-dollar deposit had been posted from an unfamiliar source. Oh fuck.

She put the phone back to her ear. "I don't know where that money came from."

"That's a good thing," she assured her. "Are you ready to help me?"

Patience's gut folded in on itself. She should call her father, ask him what to do. But she was a grown woman. A passion brought her to the Arctic, and she would protect that passion.

"Yes."

"There may come a time you have to go along with some things you normally wouldn't, but for now all I need you to do is answer my calls. It's that simple."

"That's it?" Patience dabbed at her forehead.

"Do not engage with anyone outside of your team unless they engage with you. You are not to seek out information. Do you understand that?"

"Yes."

"You're my eyes in Deadhorse. Tell me what you've seen so far."

Before a deep breath could fill and exit her lungs, Patience decided what she would and would not divulge about Forrest. Like her whales, their relationship would be guarded.

14

Better Than This

Logan ignored the shakes reminiscent of his DTs days and dug through the fruit bowl in the cafeteria. The roundest, smoothest, and brightest apple appeared. He rubbed it against his white cotton sleeve until it caught the light just right. Civilian clothes rested easy on his body. Too easy.

The governor had relieved him of his duties after dinner, but it was well into the night now.

Another man's agenda dragged him to Ana's room, spoiling all the intrigue with every step he took up to the third floor. He'd made people promises in return for an old life. Like a sheep in wolves' clothing, he'd followed the patriarch of his family, reacceptance to the pack the light at the end of the tunnel—the tunnel his cousin saw as no more than a vacuum. Logan wasn't blind to it, but he was just as empty.

He crept through the stairwell door, walked slowly

through the quiet corridor of rooms, and settled in front of Ana's door. Fist raised, he surveyed the hallway. His mouth dried, his chest tightened, and his ears rang.

You're acting like a fucking criminal.

Ana didn't need this. *Don't do this to her.*

Logan placed the apple on the ground in front of the door and took off, heart racing with his strides.

"Logan?"

He spun around.

"Where are you going?" Ana took a step into the hallway.

"Wait—"

The apple rolled beneath her foot, her striped sock feet flew into the air, and she hit the ground with a muffled curse.

He ran to her side. "Fuck. I'm sorry."

Light caramel fingers covered her face. "Just go. Please."

"Let me help you up."

Logan knelt beside her. A dainty swirl of ink snuck above her waistband, looped over her hip, then disappeared beneath her thin, baby blue long sleeve shirt. Tattoos on women didn't rub him any particular way, but he might just have to see this fluid line from beginning to end.

He scooped her up like a weightless newlywed on a destination honeymoon.

Fiery eyes glared up at him. "Seriously?"

He shrugged, the friction between their bodies fanning a fire a good man would extinguish. But he wasn't a good man and holding her was somehow easier than standing alone.

"What?" He held her tighter.

The corner of her mouth turned up. He smiled back instantly then stopped. It hurt to be happy. Teasing himself with a life he couldn't have never turned out well for Logan.

"Do you always skip class?" She gripped his shoulder and tried to lower her legs to the ground.

He kept his arm curled under her knees and the other around her back. "Sometimes."

The endless depths of her eyes reached places he shouldn't have anymore. He tried to look away but couldn't.

I need someone to know what I'm going through, but it can't be you.

"I came on a little strong this morning," Ana mumbled. "Sorry. I'm not really like that." Her gaze dropped to his chest where her fingers rubbed a bunched-up fold in his shirt. "Thank you for the apple. You don't have to stay."

He carried her across the threshold, ignoring the alarm bells between his ears. She'd come on to him just the way he'd wanted her to. A little banter. A little flirting. A little tease at the banquet. They could have made the most of Deadhorse.

"I want to be here." *Just not as someone else's puppet.* "I didn't want to wake you up if you were sleeping."

She pried away from his reluctant arms to stand on her feet. "Uh-huh."

"Really." He nudged the door shut with his foot behind them, unsure he'd accomplish what he'd come here to do, but certain she'd know the way she made him feel by the time he left. "I've been thinking about you all day."

And he had. Even with the governor and his family looming over him, he gave extra pause at the mirror, shaved for the second time, and ironed his shirt.

She pulled on the braid hanging over her shoulder. "I might have been routinely checking the peephole."

"Might have?" he chuckled.

"Maybe every thirty minutes. Fifteen minutes." She turned her shame-filled smile away.

Logan fed off her words, his old mechanics falling into place. "Tell me about that tattoo on your side."

Contrived conversation had always been a means to an end. Get women to talk about themselves to make them think he cared. Except it was different this time. Genuine. Because after tonight, he wouldn't allow himself another chance with Ana. Not after what he was about to do.

She smirked. "Are you going to tell me about yours?"

"What makes you think I have any?" He hadn't exposed any skin to her in Deadhorse.

"A guy like you..." She took him in from head to boots. "Tribal? Chinese? Some chick's name?"

He cleared his throat, ego holding strong. "I hope you're not expecting a prize from a guy like me. You fell on the last thing I gave you."

She shrugged. "Being right is prize enough."

"All right," he conceded and pulled his shirt over his head.

人

Ana gaped, wiped away the saliva pooling at the corner of her mouth. Logan sat on the edge of her desk, arms locked in his sleeves from the elbows down, his shoulders, biceps, and chest bare. Swollen muscles filled his skin, crafted by the kind of discipline and dedication sand needs to smooth rock. Fine black bands wrapped around both biceps, dragging her through an invisible, emotional mud as she approached them.

"Logan..." She brushed her fingertips across one of the faded, multi-lined bands. A simple pattern of evenly spaced dots and tiny, down-pointing arrows filled the space between the lines. The design repeated itself with the arrows pointing up. "This looks Inuit."

The tattooed lines on the backs of her grandfather's hands were one of Ana's oldest memories. She'd been detached from her family for too long. Shame from time away in the military and a failed courtship shouldn't have pushed her so far. Resistant to superstition, she'd been ignoring the signs to return home. If she was going to make something of herself in the FBI, she'd have to ignore this one too.

"It's not a half-bad story," he said.

"Tell me." She examined the identical ink on his other arm, fascinated by the imperfections from where his skin had stretched.

"I was with my shit friends the summer after high school. Wasted. On pills. Went looking to get big, meaningless tribal tattoos." He rolled his neck, took a deep breath then laughed. "Woke up with one of these on my arm and went on a warpath to find the motherfucker who did it."

Ana grinned as the memory lit up Logan's face.

"Ended up at a shady hole-in-the-wall place, met an old man named Jacob who'd free-handed it while I was passed out." Logan shook his head, gaze lost in the past. "We talked for hours. I learned a lot about the Inuit people and a lot about myself. He did the other arm while I was there."

"Have you been back since?" she asked.

His stare fell. "After I graduated from the academy. He'd passed by then, though."

"I'm sorry," she said. "I'm glad you went back for the other arm."

The past and the present mixed, darkening and aging Logan's skin. She'd been in the North Slope for weeks with no plans to take a trip to Barrow where her family was rooted.

"Thought I couldn't appreciate it without experiencing it." He stared at his arms.

"Then you must know how special it is he did this for you." Her heart warmed. "They don't share tradition with just anyone."

"I think he got the wrong guy."

"No. That's not how it works." Ana was taught to believe everything happened for a reason. Even a moment like this.

He half-smiled, head turning toward the door. Could she stop him from leaving twice? Preying on the weak link in a breaking chain ate at Ana, but she had to know where he stood for her own reasons.

Chill bumps trailed her fingers as she skimmed his bicep. "Do you like it up here?"

He smirked. "That's my line."

"It worked so well I had to try it out." Damn. She knew better than to get this close to him.

He cocked his head to the side. "I want to be nowhere.

Out of my mind for a little while."

Keep him talking.

"Your own head can be the hardest place to be," she said. "Is there something you want to talk about?"

He stared down at her tablet and room key on the desk, part of his reflection looking back in the black glass. "You ever feel like you can't win? Like you always come up short?"

She brushed at her warming cheeks. "I quit before I can lose."

His gaze shot up to hers, and she fell into an impromptu confessional. "I've left every relationship I've ever been in," she admitted. "Even the military. I thrived there, but I left the moment I realized I wasn't the best at what I did anymore."

He tossed his shirt on the desk. "Why'd you enlist?"

Swells of smooth rock rippled down his torso to his dark-wash, fitted jeans. He waited for her answer like an ad splashed against a trendy clothing store. She tried to think through his serious, unintentionally butterfly-inducing stare.

"It was," she said, inhaling his cologne, "the cheapest way to get the hell out of here."

He nodded, eyes casting down. "You ever go home?"

Ana dreaded return trips home. What she'd set out to find didn't exist yet because it was hers to make. Empty handed every time. Always looking for more, but unsure why and what exactly it was. The stars could guide her if she only had the courage to look up.

"Not as much as I should." She shrugged. "What about you? Do you ever go home?"

He shrugged. "They don't want me."

Separation. All he needed from these people was separation. Ana could work with that—convince Agent Martinez he was an innocent man and a good cop.

She leaned against the desk beside him, arm grazing his fair skin. "It doesn't look like you need them."

He lifted his head, and she could hardly stand the pained look on his face. "I need you to tell me to leave."

"Why?" she asked. What was happening to him?

"Just kick my ass out." He didn't move. "I'm no good for you."

She stared at his lips, wondering how a flawless person could be so flawed. "What about what I want?"

"That's my problem," he whispered.

She dragged her gaze up to the golden bursts in his green irises.

"I'm bound to give you whatever you want." He leaned in.

She could kiss him. Or do her job and get more intel.

Ana stepped into the open space of the room like an agent would. "My tattoo. It's a vine."

His head lolled to the side. "How far does it go?"

"Time will tell." The idea had seemed great at the time.

"So, you're adding to it. What's at the beginning?"

"A snow buttercup." Of course, she would manage to embarrass herself. Again.

He grinned. "Bright yellow?"

She nodded. "They follow the sun, and my grandmother used to say that's all I ever wanted to do."

He approached her in one slow step. "May I?"

Ana peeled down her waistband to the skin just inside her hip bone, nerves beading a sheen of sweat on her forehead. Logan took a knee, smirking as he dragged his thumb across the watercolor brush-like strokes of yellow petals. Chills radiated up her shirt.

"It's poisonous," he said.

"You know your flowers," she mumbled, waiting for his touch to vanish.

"My cousin dared me to eat one of these when I was a kid. I had a mouthful of blisters."

"Forrest?" she asked.

"No." He frowned. "His brother Sam."

"Did Forrest eat the flower too?"

"He knew better." His furrowed brow eased. "He shoved a fistful of them in Sam's mouth when he found out, though."

Ana lifted her shirt over the green swirl to the next flower. Logan's palm opened along her side beneath her rib cage to a pink peony. All she needed was a little concentration on her part and a little distraction on his. This was it.

"Sam...is he a trooper too?"

Logan bit his lip. "He's VP at Locke Industries. What's this flower for?"

"Kadena Air Force Base, Japan. I flew my first F-15 there." *Keep him talking.* "Is that a family business?"

"Forrest used to work there. He ran the place until they had a falling out." He rose slowly, hand gliding to her lower back. "This one?"

"That's..." She looked over her shoulder, face inches from his set jawline, heart hammering so loud he had to hear it. "I have no idea. I can't think."

"Orange, pointy petals."

17,000 feet. Can't breathe. Can't see.

Ana spun away from him just like the jet had that day. FBI agents weren't supposed to have triggers, weren't supposed to buckle like she did. Burning fuel singed her nose.

"Hey." Logan's voice echoed.

The room tilted on an axis it didn't have.

Land. You can do it. Land.

"I'm fine." She blinked Logan into focus.

He had a hand up as if to steady her, but she'd found her footing faster than she ever had before.

She pushed words through her sudden exasperation. "Maybe we can skip the desert flower."

He kept his gaze locked on hers, easing close enough to take her hand. "Whatever the desert flower is, it's just a stop along the way now. Right?"

A twinge of guilt dropped her head. He was trying to make her feel better, and she was trying to use him. Ana self-consoled because she didn't need anyone, but she knew damn well that wasn't the truth.

He squeezed her hand. "Right?"

"Right." She nodded.

"We all have flowers." His shoulders heaved. "You're just brave enough to wear yours."

Her body drifted to his, to the heat rolling off his skin. "I'm not as brave as you think. The vine's not about where I've been or where I'll go. It's so I can find my way back."

"I don't think you know how strong you are." He slid the hair tie at the end of her braid free. Careful fingers combed through the woven locks, coaxing Ana into a careless relaxation. "I wish I was that strong," he said.

Unruly palms skimmed up his torso, yearning to

know how someone like him was molded. "You're more than just this."

"Just what?" His fingertips grazed her scalp.

"This shell." Her breaths lost their practiced depth.

His stare flashed away, but his feet stayed planted.

Blind to her own rules, she pressed her lips to the curve of his pec, and his chest revved with a horsepower she needed to push until it was deep inside of her.

There'd be more nights for intel.

He guided her back to the desk, hands tangled in her hair and hips nudging hers with every step. Her tongue grazing the flesh over his thumping heart, she sat on the polished wood, pulling at his belt. A hot mouth fell to her neck, melding their quiet groans as a pool of euphoria spilled down her body with the pull of his lips.

"I've got to go, buttercup." He dragged his kiss along her jaw.

Quivering legs wrapped around his waist. "No," she panted.

"I can't tell you how bad I want this." He closed his eyes, and she could feel his decision before he made it.

She unlocked her ankles, reeling in clothed frustration. "You're really going to leave?"

He slid his shirt off the desk and balled up the white cotton. "It'll be the best thing I ever did for you."

Loss filled the space between them. The pink flush of his torso deepened as he backed away, climbing to his neck and face.

Ana knew better than to push. "Everybody has a past, Logan."

He swung the door open, focus ahead of him. "This has nothing to do with the past. I'm sorry."

The door shut, and Ana's room was the emptiest it had ever been, even with her own shell in it. She grabbed her tablet to document the most unsuccessful encounter she ever had with a man, wondering if the FBI felt one way or another toward sad face emojis.

Logan was a conflicted person, self-deprecating like a good man doing things he knows he shouldn't do. Before she made the call, Ana checked under the desk, behind it, along the open floor. If he had just put his shirt on and left, she wouldn't be making this phone call. Wouldn't officially be identifying him as a suspect in the FBI's investigation into the coercion of researchers in Deadhorse, Alaska.

"Martinez." Grace yawned.

"Trooper Jones was in my room tonight. He left with my room key."

"Which has direct access to Patience's room?"

"Yes." Ana covered the receiver to muffle her sigh.

"Why not use Trooper Locke? You said he's coming and going in her room like it's a damn candy shop."

Because of Snow Buttercups.

"Both Patience and Logan have confirmed there's bad blood between Forrest and the family."

"So, he leaves the corrupt family business to become a cop." She hummed for a long second. "I guess that would make mom and dad a little pissy. Either way, they're all in bed with the governor now."

"I know it won't count for anything," Ana said. "But I don't think Logan wants to be a part of this."

"It doesn't count for anything because it doesn't change anything."

She squirmed on the desktop. "I get it."

"Did you leave the key out in the open on purpose?"

Ana rubbed the tension in her brow. "There are two people between Patience and the governor. If they can't go through Forrest, they'll go through me."

Grace chuckled. "I knew I liked you."

15

Motivation

Forrest lagged behind Team October on the third floor of The Aurora Hotel after a day at sea. Patience had been distant most of the day. Stiller, Paul, and Ana were even detached, like the remainder of their time here was nothing more than punishment.

Maybe it was them. Maybe it was him. His father had dug a wormhole into Forrest's thoughts. Money did strange things to people. The loss of it did even worse things. A decent man wouldn't victimize people, let alone the ones his son cared about. But his father wasn't a decent man.

Ana bumped into Patience in the hallway. "Can I go through your room? I forgot to grab my extra key this morning."

"Did you leave one somewhere?" he asked.

She glanced back at him. "Not sure."

"Have Maria make you a new set."

"Sure thing," she mumbled.

Patience let her in the room, eyes looking up to his as she lingered in the doorway. The balance formulated itself in his mental ledger. The price was more than just expensive. A cost that changed a man.

"Goodnight." She swayed.

He opened his door, undoing his belt as he walked inside. "Give me five minutes."

She smiled and slipped into her room.

Forrest shut his door behind him, and pulled his vibrating phone from its holster. He took a deep breath.

"Hello?"

"Forrest."

He tugged at his collar. "Hi, Mom."

"You have to get out of Deadhorse."

He paused at her plea. It had been Easter the last time they'd spoken.

"I can't," he said.

"You must."

"Dad is in over his head, but you already know that."

"They're not going to hurt the girl. You can see her when this is over. Just leave."

Forrest tried to imagine a world where he abandoned the ones he cared about to spare himself. They didn't realize he operated as part of a couple now. There was no him.

"I'm not the one you should be worried about." He loosened his boots.

"You don't understand. Your father isn't in charge."

"Neither is Camden."

Her breath shook with emotion, but her voice came out clear. "I can't see you mixed up in this."

"With or without Patience, I'd still be down this road, Mom."

"I told them you wouldn't come around. They wouldn't listen to me. Said oil had been your idea years ago."

"I'm sorry things are this way." Sorry his family was this way.

"What if you convince the girl to ensure whale populations are stable at the end of her research? Everyone can win that way."

He laughed and pulled a change of clothes out of the dresser. "If there's one thing I ever learned about Dad, it's that he's your right-hand man. I know what you're doing. It's not going to work."

"This doesn't have to be hard, Forrest."

"I know."

Right or wrong didn't matter to his father when it came to his mother and vice versa. Their trust in each other was unshakable, and most importantly, profitable.

"You can stop all this whenever you want," he said.

She sighed. "It's not that easy."

"But it's supposed to be easy for me?"

"Have you thought about what's easiest for this girl you're infatuated with?"

Justice never came easy, but it was what everyone deserved, even Patience.

"Forcing her the way you try to force me? I won't do that to her."

"Whether you think it's fair or not, it's what's best for her."

"No." He refused to believe that. "These transgressions you put on people—they're toxic. They follow people their whole lives."

He couldn't escape them.

"Why is it always a fight with you?"

"You know why." He tucked the phone between his ear and shoulder and wound up the cord of his cell phone charger. "You're the one who told me I care too much."

"That you do, son. Take care of yourself out there. Please."

"Always do."

"I love you."

"Love you too, Mom." He headed for the door.

"Oh, Forrest?"

"Yeah, Mom?"

"Your father said he spoke to Logan."

Forrest's hand fell from the doorknob. Nausea punched him in the gut. Keeping Logan on the right path had always been a struggle, but Forrest had never lost faith and he never would—no matter what happened.

"Thanks, Mom."

"You're welcome."

Patience answered the door in a long sweater, bare legs, and wooly socks. A glimpse of the future placed her in his cabin, a beer in her hand inside his favorite koozie, Sunday football playing in the background. Just a lazy day together. Simple things that meant the world.

"Are you all right?" She placed a gentle hand on his arm and led him into the room.

He rubbed his head. "Just preoccupied."

My parents don't care they're hurting you, but they're going to care real soon.

"Ready to be more preoccupied?" She sat on the bed, legs tucked under her body, fingers strumming the tops of her thighs.

Behind her wide, worried eyes, wheels turned, hydroplaning into angst. He sat beside her, ready to bolt and track down whoever had put her in this state, whoever thought it was okay to steal someone's peace of mind.

She reached for his hand and gripped it tighter than she ever had before. "I need to tell you something."

"But?" He swallowed.

"I need you to let me handle it."

He stared at their hands, his chest growing tight. "Whatever it is—no."

"Remember when you said not telling you something is the same as lying?" She leaned closer, hard nipples pressing against his arm through the thin cotton.

He nodded, his waking cock keeping his words at bay.

"I have rules too. If I ask you not to do something, I need you to respect that." She guided their interlocked hands beneath the sweater, unfolding their fingers along her bare hip.

Entranced by the smooth skin under his palm, enthralled by the control of her small hand on top of his, he almost agreed.

"This distracting superpower of yours," he exhaled a heavy breath, "is only going to get you so far, honey."

She slid his hand between her legs, cupped herself with it and forced his middle finger inside of her. His dick twitched. It could be soaking up her hot, wet pussy right now.

"Fuck, Patience."

He tore himself away, paced to the wall where a

small framed picture of an Arctic fox hung, and counted the beats of his heart, unable to lower it.

"Say you'll let me handle it and get over here," she said.

He turned around, the first wave of adrenaline spilling across his skin. Two fingers moved in slow circles over her clit as she squeezed her breast, carrying on without him.

"Tell me," he demanded.

She spread her thighs wider.

"Fine." He pressed the heel of his palm down his erection.

"Fine what?" she asked.

"I'll let you handle it," he lied.

After the slightest squint of her eyes, she reached for him, and he moved like a magnet to metal. He kissed her with the gentleness of an apology, deceit overcoming his will power.

She stared up at him, the corner of her bottom lip disappearing between her teeth.

She knows you're lying.

"I'm ten thousand dollars richer," she said. "Someone deposited money into my account. I'm not sure who, but I have a fairly good idea."

They'd made their first move on Patience. Time was leaving Forrest's side with every passing hour now, making the hunter feel hunted. He had to stop this.

Forrest took the chair from the desk, spun it around to face Patience and sat, elbows planted on his knees and fingers threaded together. "I can't promise I'll stay out of this."

He would always do everything he could.

She gazed at the empty space on the bed where he'd been. "I need you by my side."

"I am." *Why couldn't she see that?*

"No, you're in a chair across the room getting ready to interrogate me. Again."

It was more than just protecting Patience. It was preserving her power, dignity, and conscience. Locke Industries had taken all of that away from him and he fought like hell to get it back. He wouldn't see her in that fight.

"The man that sits right there," He pointed beside her, "Operates on feelings, not facts. He's irrational. He's..." Forrest tried to take a deep breath.

Patience eased off the bed, her feet light on the ground as she came to him and straddled his lap. "He's the man I met in Chicago."

Forrest wrapped his arms around her waist, shaking his head. If he always did the right thing, he would never have to bend—to anyone.

"You trusted me in Chicago," she said.

"You changed my life in Chicago." The words came out before he could stop them.

He'd lost control of the conversation so quickly.

She grabbed his face, forcing him to look her in the eyes. "We have to get through October because I don't want just November and December with you. I want it all."

Puzzle pieces of his life were just waiting to connect, and he couldn't shake the fear that they would be jumbled all over again.

He rubbed her back in slow, big circles, the motion taking the edge off the knot at the back of his throat.

"Leave Deadhorse. When this is all over, I'll go to Anchorage. Hell, I'll go to North Carolina if that's where you want to be."

She smiled, tears welling up in her eyes. "Would you leave with me? Right now?"

He couldn't look at her. They both knew the answer.

"If I had half a mind, I would take you up on that."

She locked her arms around his neck. "I'm not ready to leave."

"Then let me do something." He brought her as close as he could, smothering himself in the faint vanilla on her skin.

"I can't."

Tension built across Forrest's shoulders. "You haven't heard from any of Camden's people? No one's reached out to you? Anyone?"

She leaned back, her brow forming a V. "No."

He placed her swiftly on the bed. "I need to make some calls."

"No." She jumped to her feet and grabbed his hand. "We're not even sure where the money is from. Forrest don't...you can't..."

"Why?" he demanded. "Why tell me if you don't want me to do anything about it?"

"Because."

He tried to ignore the stomp of her foot, the red in her cheeks, and the long sleeves of her sweater that kept falling down her arms. Cuteness didn't warrant authority.

"Why?" he pressed. "You want me to know in case something happens to you? Is that it?"

The thought of any harm coming to her only made

his choice clearer.

"No." Her shoulders fell with an exasperated sigh. "In case something happens to you."

"Me?" He blinked.

"You put yourself between me and them." Her head fell to the side. "How can I not tell you? How can I leave you unprepared like that?"

What? Forrest's hand froze around his phone. Heat surged his cheeks as he grappled with a loss for words. He took care of people. They didn't take care of him. What was she thinking?

"Don't worry about me," he said. "I need you to concentrate on yourself."

"I need you to listen to me."

He slid his phone back into his pocket and cautiously retook his seat on the bed. His heart wanted to listen, believed this could be the right thing to do, but his mind wasn't so convinced.

"If Camden is behind this, you'll be the first to know." She rested a hand on his shoulder. "Right now, we just need to wait and see what happens. And if going along with it—"

"No, Patience. That's sticky ground."

"No matter what, I just need you to trust me."

Forrest took her hand from his shoulder, bringing it to his lips. "Don't think for a second I don't trust you."

I just couldn't live with myself if anything happened.

She threaded her fingers through his hair, dragging her fingernails over his scalp. "The bank is going to call me back tomorrow. They said the money came from an account in Hawaii. It's a start."

He slowed the graze of his fingertips along her wrist.

A small bank in Honolulu held his buyout money from Locke Industries. There would be one call he had to make.

16

Deviations

Patience scooped a second helping of scrambled eggs onto her plate in the cafeteria buffet line. Just as she reached for the bacon tongs, a man slipped ahead of her.

"Morning, Patience." The governor winked, stirring the syrup beside the French toast.

Oh shit.

Agent Martinez had said not to seek him out, but here he was, blocking the pancakes.

"Morning." She cleared her throat, hoping to shake the squeak out of it.

"I'm just dying to know if my gesture was too grand," he said, pouring the sweet brown liquid onto a half-eaten piece of French toast. "We probably should have discussed it, but I just love surprises."

Patience squirmed. Breakfast chatter drowned out the diner-filled cafeteria. His grin hijacked her senses, made her zone in like he was the guard and she was the prisoner.

"The money." Of course, it had been him, but now it was real.

He shrugged. "Buy yourself something nice."

"I can't accept it."

"Yes, you can." He chuckled. "Be like my wife and spend it all on shoes."

Every now and again Patience fancied something outside of the wardrobe staples. Sure, her closet at home had some standouts, but life didn't revolve around items—or money.

"How about this." He moved her gently aside so one of his assistants could pass them in line. "You help me pick out a pair of Louboutins for my wife, and we'll call it even."

"What do you really want from me?" She eased back, his hand still on her elbow.

"Just a slight deviation."

Here it comes.

"Deviation?" she asked.

"You know what I'm doing in Deadhorse." He stared through her, never blinking. "You help me, and I'll get you much more than money. You can do your own research. Aerial, marine. However you like it and wherever you want it."

The little power-hungry bulb in the back of her brain dimmed as fast as it glowed. "You expect to get away with that?"

"Absolutely."

Patience shuffled her feet. Forrest's dark hair rose above the crowd, heading her way.

"This deviation, what makes you think I can do it?"

"I know you can."

She cleared her throat again. "But what if I won't."

He smiled, the hand on her elbow moving to her shoulder. "If the whales cooperate, you may not have to do anything at all. I just need someone in my corner during this final stretch. Someone to help me do what I think is best for the people of Alaska."

Patience wouldn't drink the Kool-Aid, but she wouldn't put herself in harm's way again. "I—"

"Pumps?" The governor asked. "Or what are those things called? Stilettos?" A wild glint shone in his eyes.

Heat radiated off Forrest's body as he stepped in front of her. The governor disappeared behind the wall of tense muscle.

"This is over," Forrest said.

Patience froze behind his back. The cafeteria quieted and heads turned their way.

"What do you think you're doing Trooper Locke?" Camden muttered.

Agent Martinez would want to know about this. Patience had danced around Forrest's presence when Mitchell broke into her room. Had said he was following up on the altercation with Stiller. Would a man just doing his job call for the scene that was unfolding?

"This is your first and last warning. Do not communicate with Ms. Cline." The solidarity in his voice only strengthened with his words. "Are we clear?"

"You need to listen to your father." Camden's whisper came out hard and heavy with intent. "That badge is going to get you killed."

"Are. We. Clear?"

"Do you know what you're throwing away?"

"Do you?"

Commotion came from the coffee stand. Logan snatched a wad of napkins as the crowd snickered at his curses over a spilled thermos.

"Stilettos," Patience blurted.

Forrest stared back over his shoulder, and the governor leaned around him, smiling.

"A matching clutch wouldn't hurt." She swallowed.

"See, Trooper Locke." Camden pointed at her. "Pay was just helping me pick out an anniversary present for my wife."

Worry flooded Forrest's eyes. "You got your answer. Time to fly, Patience."

They headed outside with the rest of Team October, Patience following Forrest's heavy footsteps through the snow. The crunch of his boots echoed in the still morning air, much louder than her teams' banter and the fume-spewing trucks barreling by.

Her bank wouldn't open until 8:00 a.m. eastern, pushing back her inquiries to after the days' survey. She wouldn't get her father involved unless she had to.

The ball was still in her court even if Forrest didn't want it to be. If the governor had Corey beaten to an inch of his life, what would he do to Forrest?

During her phone call to Agent Martinez tonight, she'd have to explain Forrest's need to know about the FBI investigation. It could keep him from doing something stupid. It could save his life.

⋀

Forrest juggled incessant nausea and absolute rage while donning his flight gear in the airport locker room. After

Patience had fallen asleep, he'd checked the balance on his savings account in Honolulu. He was ten grand poorer.

They were burying him. One massive conspiracy by Locke Industries, helmed by a man who didn't have a damn thing on the line. The governor had set himself up for a clean getaway.

"Patience, I need to speak to you." He zipped the back of his orange suit up.

Ana took her time following Stiller out the locker room, openly studying Forrest from head to toe. "We're out in five."

"Got it," he snapped.

Patience stayed by the women's lockers. "Yes?"

"What did Camden—"

"It was him." She crossed her arms awkwardly in the bulky suit. "The money came from him."

Forrest nodded so hard his body rocked. "In exchange for what?"

"A stable whale population at the end of October."

The world dropped its weight on Forrest. "This is over. Now."

She stood tall. "It's not your call."

"Like hell, it's not." His voice bounced off the walls and back at him.

Where did she get the nerve to tell him what to do? It was time he took over Deadhorse.

"If the whales cooperate, I won't have to do anything."

There it was again. The lying by omission. The lack of responsibility. The easy way out.

"But you understand that's because of all the MMOs before you?" He slammed his locker door shut. She was better than this. "He got to them, and now he's getting to you."

"If he's getting to anyone, it's you. I don't have to do anything for him yet." She shrugged. "If that time comes...well, I'll cross that bridge when I get to it."

"You're already halfway across the bridge, Patience." He bent over and braced himself against the bench bolted to the floor, ready to tear it free. The play was clear. There was no more *wait and see*. Camden had a hold of Forrest, and he couldn't admit it aloud.

"What are you going to do? Blow this whole thing up?"

"I'll do what I have to." If he didn't, he'd be tied to this forever.

"I heard what he said, Forrest." Her foot tapped against the ground. "About that badge getting you killed."

He patted his chest, his heart pulsing against his palm in agreement. "He has no idea what my badge means to me."

"But *I* do." She blew hair out of her eyes, tone loud and searing.

Disbelief colored her face in a foreign shade. She couldn't see what he saw. Couldn't see the reality he was living.

"Then you should understand—"

"No," she bit out. "You're the one who doesn't understand. If I do what he wants, there won't be any consequences."

A sliver of doubt crossed him like a breeze. So subtle. So unlike him and everything he's ever known.

"Patience, if I let him get away with this, we'll be

bound to him forever. That's a consequence."

She walked to the door shaking her head and held it open for him. "If it keeps you safe, it's a consequence I'm willing to live with."

Forrest kept his ground, a divide growing not between him and Patience, but within himself. He should tell her where the money came from. He should tell her he doesn't know how to operate with her feelings all around him. He should trust her.

But he couldn't.

"I'll be here when you get back," he said.

With silent, parted lips and disappointment-filled eyes, she left.

17

Goodbye

The Twin Otter plane rumbled over Forrest's head, flashing passed the sun as he headed for his Tahoe. He sat in the driver's seat, called his bank in Honolulu, and reported the missing funds. Someone had created a checking account in his name, transferred ten thousand dollars from his savings into it, and then sent it to an account in Charlotte, North Carolina before closing it.

Just like that, it looked as if not only Locke Industries paid Patience off, but him on their behalf. If they knew he met Patience prior to Deadhorse, they could chalk it up to the initial encounter of their plan.

Forrest wiped a hand over his face in the icy car. He drafted a memo to his captain outlining his findings, his concerns, and the department's need to open an investigation into Governor Camden. After his millionth read-through, he attached Mitchell's arresting report as his first piece of evidence then promised an affidavit from Patience corroborating his story.

He checked the Tahoe's tire pressure in every wheel, took a lap around The Aurora Hotel, and was backing into a parking space when the call came in.

"Hello?" he answered, breakfast climbing up his throat.

"Are you fucking kidding me?" his captain asked.

"No, sir," he swallowed.

"I have to ask you again. Are you fucking kidding me?"

"No, I understand it's a lot to take in."

"A lot?" he asked. "A lot? You've lost your goddamn mind."

Forrest closed his eyes to offset the dizziness. "It's all true."

"I understand you've had a hard year, and you might be going through some midlife crisis right now, but this is career suicide."

"You're saying you don't believe me?"

"Regardless of the truth, this is a political nightmare. The money you're out is a drop in the ocean compared to the legal fees you're going to incur defending yourself. You understand an investigation into the governor is an investigation into you, Logan, and Locke Industries."

"I understand that."

"Are you prepared to lose that fight?"

Forrest tossed his hat into the passenger seat. "Lose? I haven't done anything wrong. They've hurt people. They're going to hurt people. It's my responsibility to stop this."

"They'll out lawyer you. They'll bury you. Believe me, Governor Camden will not let you do this to him."

"They're intimidating, coercing, and assaulting researchers to sway scientific data their way. This is bigger than the governor."

"Forrest, listen." The captain's panicked voice lost its edge. "I wish every trooper I had was like you. My respect and loyalty for you, you know where it lies. I'm behind you 100%, but you have to understand what's at stake here."

"I understand. If I had no intention on following through with this, I would have never brought it to you."

"All right," he said. "Fine. I can't promise you anything, but if you can get me that sworn statement from the MMO, maybe I can get it in front of a judge."

Victory swallowed his fears. "You got it."

⅄

Patience welcomed Forrest's distant escort back to The Aurora Hotel from the airport hangar. A day of flying had left her to narrow down her options, and him all the time to do whatever he wanted without her knowledge or consent.

She ignored the stubborn man all the way up to her room. Once no one was around, they'd have to approach the fork in the road. He headed one way and she another.

Patience entered her room and shut the door behind her, breathing in the slightest hint of peppermint.

She dumped her gear on the bed and turned into the cool barrel of a silencer against her cheek. A scream wouldn't leave her lips no matter how hard she tried.

Familiar eyes stared down the pistol. Clean-shaven, fresh haircut, minty breath. She almost didn't recognize him in a navy fleece pullover, stonewashed jeans, and shiny, black leather boots.

Mitchell held a finger to his lips. Her pulse stomped between her ears and little speckles of light danced in her peripheral. She nodded.

"Put your laptop on the desk."

His aim followed her motions like a fatal dance between lovers, the anticipatory strike looming but never coming.

Mitchell sat in the desk chair. "Come here."

She froze.

He patted his thigh. "Sit."

Hairs rose all over Patience's body. The smelly, oil-covered worker had escaped his jail cell in Barrow and found his way back to her room to scare her, to threaten her all over again.

She hovered over his knee, squeezed her eyes shut and sat. Strange arms circled around her waist.

"How are you here?" she whispered.

"Called in a favor to a friend." He powered on the laptop.

"And in my room?"

He fixed the collar on her jacket. "Same friend. A mutual one matter of fact."

His smile grew as he waited for her to connect the dots. "C' mon. You're not as stupid as you look."

"The governor?" She curled into her body as tightly as she could.

He sighed. "You think he gets his hands dirty?"

Someone in law enforcement could get him out of jail. It couldn't be Forrest, though.

Ana's key was missing.

"It's not Trooper Jones..."

He grinned.

Patience stared at the ceiling, tears pricking her eyes. "What do you want?"

"I need your passwords, and then I'll do the rest."

"I spoke to Camden. He said—"

"He said you're going to help us so you shouldn't have an issue with us monitoring your computer." His arms tightened as she recoiled.

Patience grasped her cold hands together. Maybe Forrest would come. Maybe it was better he didn't. The light beneath the door glowed without disruption.

"Forrest isn't coming." He chuckled. "He's got a flat tire on his Tahoe. Probably picked up a nail driving around Deadhorse today talking on the phone. You know who he made all those calls to?"

Patience shook her head. "No."

"You know we're going to have a problem if Forrest gets out of line, right?"

"I can't control Forrest," she muttered.

"There are ways to control a man." He lifted the pistol. "And you don't want me to be the one to do it."

The magic number shined on the bottom corner of the screen. If she didn't call Agent Martinez in fifteen minutes, she'd call the room pretending to be Brenda.

"Let's get this over with," she begged.

He grabbed her face with one hand, pulling it down to him. "You know, I thought you would be happy to see me."

Mitchell had shaven years off along with his scraggly beard, but he hadn't lost the glint in his eye from that night.

She wrenched her jaw free. "Don't touch me."

Denim locked around her legs and one hand snatched both of her wrists. Weight greater than his own held her down.

Hot peppermint blew into her hair. "Until this job is done, you're going to be seeing me whether you like it or not."

"Let me log in so you can do whatever you have to do."

He released her with a shove, and she bounced on the bed. "Password. Now."

Patience gave Mitchell access to the research. It burned. Rubbed her in the worst way. Even though she had the FBI in her back pocket, the corruption over-taking her computer reeked of failure.

Mitchell typed away, plugging in code beyond her IT knowledge under her user name. She'd never felt so used before.

He closed the laptop. "Until next time."

"There doesn't need to be a next time."

He removed a cell phone from his pocket, his smirk melting away. "Hello?"

Patience squirmed under his hardening glare.

"I understand." Mitchell lowered the phone then stretched his neck. "Pay, we have a little problem."

Patience inched back on the bed.

"It seems an MMO from July's survey has been called for questioning by the Alaska State Troopers." Mitchell's nose twitched. "I think we know who's behind this."

"I haven't spoken to Forrest today." She held a hand up like it could stop a bullet.

"Listen." He knelt in front of the bed and snatched her hand. "I don't like to kill people. It's messy, and I've been masquerading as a roughneck long enough."

Patience strained to pull her hand away. "I'll talk to him."

He squeezed her knuckles. "I could get you out of here in a piece of luggage. Easy. Forrest, now he's a different story, and since I just got these boots, I really don't want to scuff them up already."

Patience tried to breathe between the spurts of pain shooting down her fingers. "I'll talk to him."

Mitchell eased his grasp and caressed her pink flesh. "I'll give you two days. That's it."

"He can be stubborn."

Bones met, crunching beneath her skin. She bit back a curse and a whimper.

"Get him on board. I keep my shoes clean, and you get to go home to Sunset Beach for Thanksgiving."

She nodded. "All right."

He patted her throbbing hand. "Get some ice for that."

Patience barricaded herself in the bathroom the moment the door closed behind Mitchell. Tonight, she'd ask the FBI for something in return. If they could get her out of Deadhorse in twenty-four hours, then they could get Forrest out too.

$$\wedge$$

Forrest lowered the SUV, threw the jack in the back and rushed inside The Aurora Hotel. A flat tire had spooked him, threatened his only mode of transportation, but it had taken too long. He left her alone for too long.

The research team entered the lobby. Heaving breaths settled into deep ones, the snow melted in his hair, and time returned to his side.

Patience hung back as they went into the cafeteria. She looked at Forrest almost like he wasn't there, like he wasn't real. Those wheels behind her pretty eyes spun so fast.

"I'm sorry," he blurted. "The hotel manager called—"

"Flat tire." She bit her lip. "I know."

He pointed to a flyer pinned to the wall. "Aurora Borealis tonight. I know you want to see it. I thought we could talk."

"We have a lot to talk about." Soft lines creased her forehead. "I need you to hear me out, Forrest. Now."

"And I need you to do the same."

He followed her to the fireplace in the den and sat beside her on the warm hearth.

"I know you've thought about everything." She pulled her sleeves down over Carolina Panther blue knit gloves and wrapped her arms around her body. "But I have to ask you to stop what you're doing. For me."

Flames warming his back overwhelmed the cold. There was no stopping. He had an investigation to run.

"I can't do that," he said.

"I need you to know something before I say what I have to say then."

"Wait." He didn't want his heart tossed in the fire. "Don't make this about us."

"I care about you very much." Her voice broke.

"No." He stood, even though he had nowhere to run to.

"Stop what you're doing, or we're done."

He shuffled backward until he bumped a rocking chair. This wasn't a part of his plan. It wasn't how things were supposed to go.

"We're going to get through this," he promised.

"You have to trust me, and we both know—"

"This isn't fair, Patience."

She rose from the fire. "You've got until the northern lights to figure out what you're going to do."

He blocked her path. "My captain knows everything. We stand a chance at taking Camden down, but I can't do it without you."

She closed her eyes for a moment, tugging a glove off her hand. Knuckles too swollen to bend and discolored skin slipped free of the knitted fabric. "Mitchell is back. I need you to stop, and I need you to do it for me."

She walked around him like the calm leading the storm to shore, and he followed her to the cafeteria with only one target in sight.

Logan.

Forrest barreled through the swinging kitchen doors and there his cousin stood in the grease-filled air, stuffing his face with French fries.

"What?" Logan caught half-chewed potatoes falling out of his mouth.

Blind rage scratched at Forrest. "Start praying."

Logan blinked. "Just calm down a second."

Forrest swung. A jaw cracked against his fist. Logan's palms slapped the tile floor as he broke his fall.

"God damn." Logan spit blood.

"How *could* you," Forrest yelled between his teeth. "You stole Ana's key, didn't you? You let them get to Patience."

Logan leaned on his knee, tried to stand, but fell back down. "They promised nobody was going to get hurt."

"They hurt her. That son of a bitch crushed her hand, but you probably already knew he was back here."

"They got to me, man. I'm sorry."

Forrest dragged him to his feet. "No, you let them get to you."

Everybody in the world had lined up against Forrest.

"You're going to get yourself killed." Logan coughed. "And if something happens to Patience, that's on you."

"Fuck you." Forrest let go fistfuls of his cousin's jacket. "I'm the only person doing what needs to be done."

After a wobble, Logan found steady footing. "You're so selfish and you don't even see it. People who care about you, people you're supposed to care about, are asking you, begging you to stop, but you won't."

"None of you realize you're handing your lives over to Camden forever." He shook his head. "There's no fucking difference."

"I'm getting my old life back." Logan's eyes watered.

"The one where you drink yourself to death? Where you're a pawn for the rest of your life?"

"All I know is, I'm not the most powerful man in the room, never have been. You need to forget what that feels like and salvage what you can."

Forrest's phone buzzed to life. His captain's name flashed up at him.

"Is that Thompson?" Logan asked. "Call him off. Now."

He sent the call to voicemail. "After everything we've been through, Logan."

"You're not going to get Camden. You're chasing a ghost. You're going to make Locke Industries pay for this. That's me. That's you. That's our family."

"That *was* my family." The kitchen doors swung closed behind Forrest.

With his eyes back on Patience, he planted his phone to his ear and listened to Captain Thomson's message.

"Forrest, I followed up on that Mitchell Wilson. His bond hearing was bumped up. Logan's name is on the docket. Someone's pulling strings. Get me that statement. I want it in audio, video, and writing. ASAP. And Forrest, you keep Logan in the dark until further notice."

18

Morning Shift

Patience turned the shower on and dialed Agent Martinez. Ana would be banging on her door any second to watch the northern lights. Hairs kept rising on her arms like a spirit brushing her skin. The sensation had been looming since Mitchell's return.

"Patience." Agent Martinez spoke calmly through the line. "We considered all the information you provided us with."

Patience half chuckled, half choked. "Your nonchalance is really encouraging. I think I'm going to be sick. You can't leave him out here."

"The FBI is denying your request to evac Forrest out of Deadhorse."

"We need to at least tell him about the FBI's investigation," Patience pled. "He's going to blow this thing wide open."

"You cannot tell him anything about your

involvement with the FBI. That is something you've already agreed to. It could compromise everything."

"He's launched his own investigation. Doesn't that compromise everything?"

"There's a reason we're not pulling him out of Deadhorse."

"Tell me why."

Agent Martinez huffed. "That ten thousand dollars in your bank account, it came from an account belonging to Forrest Locke."

"What?" Patience turned the volume up on her phone.

"We have surveillance footage of you with him in Chicago from August. I know you haven't been entirely forthcoming about your relationship with Trooper Locke, but you're a smart girl, and you've been making smart decisions in Deadhorse."

"Hold on," Patience said. "What are you saying?"

"Forrest Locke is under investigation by the FBI. There are too many connecting dots, Patience. We can't ignore them."

"I sat beside him at that bar. Nature grounded that flight. Governor Camden put him in Deadhorse."

"I understand that this is difficult to hear."

"Difficult? It's all one big set up."

"Which is why you have to see this to the end. Camden can't roll when the shit hits the fan and let Locke Industries take the fall because you tie him to everything."

"Forrest is going to ask for a statement tonight."

"You know you can't give it to him."

"That won't stop him."

"Let him prove his innocence."

"If they kill him, you'll know he's innocent, is that it?"

"He's entirely capable of taking care of himself. Don't forget he used to run Locke Industries."

"Yeah, but he's not like them."

Patience pressed the end button and dropped her phone on the counter. It caught the edge of the dry sink and slipped in. Forrest needed out of Deadhorse—right now.

∧

The unnatural glow of the Prudhoe Bay oil fields shadowed the stargazers scattered across the icy field off Deadhorse's main road. Workers, tourists, politicians, researchers—they were all under the same sky for the same reasons. Governor Camden strolled by, whistling at the dancing lights. Patience trusted Forrest to keep an eye on him as she lost herself in the earth's wonder.

Green bled into the crystal black sky with gentle strokes of a luminescent paintbrush, stretching across the stars, across the end of the world.

"Wow." She reached for the phenomenon, the moving colors, the quiet song. Unattainable in her palm but touching her soul.

"It's like magic," she whispered.

"It's beautiful," he said.

She smiled at Forrest, lost in a moment outside their reality. "You're not even looking at the sky."

"Looking at you is better."

She held her hand out, and he took it in front of the team, in front of Camden, in front of everyone. Every moment should be shameless, painless, and honest. Good memories to cherish and bad ones to learn from. She may not leave Deadhorse with Forrest, but she wouldn't leave with regrets either.

An icy breeze caressed her cheek, coaxing the words out. "I can't help you."

I won't let them hurt you.

"I've got a new lead." He brought her closer, wrapping an arm around her back. "I know there's going to be more. Please, your testimony is everything. Paul won't talk to me and I can't get a hold of Corey."

Patience squeezed his hand and held it to her chest. "I meant what I said earlier."

The emerald in his eyes dueled with the colors above. "We're not over."

"Are you stopping your investigation?"

"I can't." He grimaced. "And I won't."

The shutter of lenses, the tail end of murmurs and bewildered gasps filtered around them.

She stood on her tiptoes and pulled him down to kiss his lips. Even though she'd known he'd be this way, it ripped a hole in the beautiful night sky she couldn't fix.

Panic filled his glistening eyes. "Please. It doesn't have to be this way."

"I'm giving Camden what he wants." She smiled through the lump in her throat. "I don't expect you to forgive me."

He shook his head. "My family is doing this to you. Let me stop it."

"It's not your fault." She would never blame him. "Even if you walk away."

Hard lines crossed out the last bit of doubt on his

face. "I'll never walk away."

It wasn't in him to let go, but she'd do it for him.

"I'm walking away." She stepped back, dropping his hand. "You might hate me tomorrow."

"I could never hate you," he vowed.

She wouldn't cry. She'd save the tears for four in the morning when she couldn't take it anymore. "Bye, Forrest."

⋏

Forrest spent the night guarding Patience's door, and the morning trying to reach his captain. Nothing. Worry stole his focus, distracted him from the goal. Camden and Locke Industries would answer to the Alaska State Troopers. They'd taken too much from Patience and far too much from him. Even if it meant Logan went down, then so be it. Justice could be blindfolded, but that same blindfold could be lifted.

Weather grounded the research team to the hotel's first-floor conference room, so he hovered about, scheming, planning, thinking. Patience would have to come around if they stood a chance at getting Camden. He'd vouch for her when the time came, testify on her behalf. She was innocent in all this too. He'd do anything for the woman he loved.

He paced the length of the table the researchers had cluttered with their maps and graphs till silence cut across the conference room. Patience and her team lifted their heads. Forrest whipped toward the door, hand on his pistol. Captain Thompson stared back at him.

"Trooper Locke, I need to see you outside for a minute," he said. "Trooper Andrews will stand watch."

Energized hope sent Forrest through the door. For his captain to come all the way to Deadhorse, there must have been a major development.

Today was the day.

Snow poured in gusts of high winds outside The Aurora Hotel. Forrest followed his captain to the marked SUVs.

Captain Thompson watched a tractor-trailer barrel past then turned to Forrest. "Patience Cline."

"She's refusing to provide me with a statement," Forrest said. "I don't think she's a lost cause, but we may need to turn our efforts elsewhere. Mitchell Wilson is here."

Captain Thompson nodded, a strange look coming over his face. "Did you put your hands on her?"

He reared back. "What?"

"You heard me, Forrest." The captain squinted in the icy air. "Did you put your hands on Patience Cline?"

"Absolutely not." His breath shot out in a fog. "Why are you asking me this?"

"This." He held up an image on his phone. "Did you do this?"

Patience's swollen, bruised hand filled the screen.

"Mitchell did that to her." He jabbed his finger at the phone.

"We've been looking for him since we got here," Captain Thompson said. "He's not here."

Forrest's world spun. "I'm telling you the truth."

"It's your word against hers right now."

"What?" His brain went into overdrive as dark clouds swirled above Deadhorse.

"I'm sorry, Forrest. I'm going to have to—"

Fresh snow flew behind Forrest as he ran to the hotel's entrance and shoved a fellow trooper aside. Everything he had lay like shattered glass in his mind. Bodies shuffled out of his way as he stormed to the conference room. Trooper Andrews met him at the doorway. Forrest laid his shoulder into him, knocking his friend onto his back.

All the researchers huddled together except for Patience. She stood alone across the oblong table, tears streaking down her face.

"Tell me you didn't," he shouted. "*Tell me.*"

This couldn't be happening. They were going to arrest him.

"I did." She wiped her face, shoulders shaking. "I did. I'm sorry."

"How could you?" Betrayal cut through him, breaking him into half a man.

"You gave me no choice."

The person he fought for, the person who'd brought him back to life, had taken it all. "This is all I have, Patience."

Trooper Andrews wrenched Forrest's arms behind his back, but there was no point in fighting. He'd already lost.

She came around the table. "You wouldn't stop."

"I love you." He couldn't bear to look at her, dropping his head. "How could you do this to me?"

How did he let this happen?

Patience's sobs mixed with the reading of Forrest's Miranda Rights.

"I don't want to ever see you again," he croaked.

Guests hushed and shuffled as Forrest was led

from the hotel. Restrained by a colleague, accused by a superior—a nightmare he could have never dreamed of or thought possible. He rode to the airport in the back of his SUV beside his cousin while Trooper Andrews drove, and Captain Thompson rode shotgun.

Trooper Andrews rubbed his neck. "Did you really have to tackle my ass? One assault charge is enough don't you think?"

"She lied." Forrest stared at his boots.

Just when he'd found a foot to stand on, it was gone. He hadn't done his job, and Patience had taken any chance of retrying away from him.

"She was remorseful, I'll say that." Trooper Andrews turned to the captain.

"Paid leave while we investigate her allegations. Okay, Forrest?" Captain Thompson said.

"What exactly are those allegations?" he asked.

Captain Thompson sighed. "That you were intimidating her into agreeing with a statement she did not agree with against Governor Camden. She tried to get away from you, but you wouldn't let her go, resulting in the injuries to her hand."

"She did what she had to," Logan said. "We all did."

"I don't want to hear another fucking word out of you." Forrest turned to his cousin.

"Forrest," Dawson Andrews met eyes with him in the rearview mirror, "you can tell the captain about Patience, or I can."

Dawson had seen more than just the dissolution of Forrest's career, but Forrest couldn't say it, couldn't get the lump in his throat to go down.

"He's in a relationship with Patience," Dawson said.

Forrest didn't recognize his own scratchy voice. "She ended that relationship today. I would never put hands on her, but this is going to follow me for the rest of my life."

"You should have listened to her," Logan bit down on his lip. "You should have listened to me."

They'd be sitting in Deadhorse helping to facilitate a crime if he'd listened to them. "You wouldn't be wearing that uniform if it wasn't for me."

"I'm not going to be wearing it much longer."

"You're no better than Sam." Forrest blinked back the tears. "It's a goddamn shame."

Logan wiped his face on his shoulder.

"Listen." Captain Thompson whipped around in his seat. "Trooper Jones, we're performing a conduct review. You're suspended without pay until further notice."

"The researchers?" Logan asked. "You've got troopers with them?"

"Andrews will stay back. The governor declined a replacement for his security detail."

"Stay out of his way, Dawson." Logan dropped his head again. "That way everyone comes home safe."

"Forrest," Captain Thompson said, turning back toward the road, "you've made it hard on me, son. No matter what happens, I'm going to have to ask you to sit this one out."

"Even if the charges are dropped?"

"Even if the charges are dropped."

Forrest nodded. "I understand, Joe."

The snow stopped as they pulled into the airport. Forrest

tried not to look back as he climbed out of the Tahoe, but he could see The Aurora Hotel in the distance, feel the drop in temperature.

"No hard feelings, man?" Trooper Andrews released one of Forrest's wrists and brought his hands around to cuff them in the front.

Forrest had found teenage, runaway Dawson Andrews in the woods after a fight with his foster father during his first year on the job. Forrest had helped him become a wildlife trooper after college and then supported his transfer to the highway patrol. They lifted in the gym together, always lending an ear to the other when they needed to unload a rough day.

"Of course not. Joe brought you because he knows I trust you."

"And your trust is pretty shaken about now."

Forrest swallowed. "I've never been blind-sided like that in my life."

Emotion spilled through his veins, riding a weak moment like the first big swells of the year. He leaned back against the Tahoe.

"I didn't mean to bust your balls back there. I was just thinking down the road if you get a chance to testify against Camden, they're going to tear your motive all to hell."

"Between her," He couldn't even say her name, "and my family, yeah."

"I'll look after your girl." Dawson led them around the Tahoe. "But I'm going to keep my ears open, all right? You're not going down like this."

19

Butane

Patience kept the candle snug in her coat, traversing the frozen mud through swirls of exhaust fumes to the Deadhorse Arctic Ocean Shuttle. The cloud ceiling was too low to fly again, so the team followed as the governor and his goons passed thundering tractor-trailers for a special trip. The shuttle, the only means to see the oil company owned beaches, didn't operate after September for the everyday man. This would be Patience's only chance to speak with her mother on the rocky shore, to feel the place where the land met the sea.

All thanks to a man she despised.

Ana linked their arms. "You haven't said a word since yesterday."

Trooper Andrews loomed behind them, his alliance to Forrest bleeding through his stoic demeanor.

"There's not a whole lot to say." She held Ana's arm tighter.

"I know why you did what you did," she whispered.

Patience looked at her friend, her face fierce in its smooth, high cheekbone beauty. "Nobody else does."

"When this is over, I'm going to help you make sure everyone knows."

"It's worse than I thought." She couldn't afford to hurt anyone else. "I don't want you mixed up in this."

Ana upped their pace, pulling them well ahead of Trooper Andrews. "You may be the eyes in Deadhorse, but I'm the ears."

Chills poured down Patience's skin as Agent Martinez's words echoed through her mind.

"But you don't know that. Got it?"

Patience wasn't alone. She hadn't been the entire time. "Yes."

Ana released her arm and shoved her hands in her pockets. "We're going to get these bastards."

Patience slowed, hope and relief making her eyes water. The team walked ahead to meet the governor and his minions. Trooper Andrews appeared by her side, his stare cutting through her with surgeon-like precision.

"Problem?" he asked.

She smiled. "I just want you to know everything is going to be all right."

Warm air blew from between his lips, rising in a white fog. "I don't know what kind of game you think you're playing, but you've got a man's life in your hands."

"I do." She patted his arm and headed toward the shuttle. "But it's not the one you think."

Governor Camden waited for them to board before climbing the steps into the rumbling bus. Patience slid all the way to the window in her seat and he slid in right behind her, patting her leg with a leather-clad hand. Trooper Andrews squinted from his spot near the driver, words hanging from his lips but never coming out.

Governor Camden nudged her shoulder. "Quite a scene yesterday."

"I end all my relationships that way." She wiped at the dusty glass.

"A little public for my tastes," he mused. "But there's not much else you can do with a stubborn, righteous man like Forrest than condemn him and strip him of what little power he did have."

Patience gripped the seat in front of her as they descended the uneven road. Camden didn't sway with the rock of the shuttle, though, bound by a force he believed was stronger than hers, deeper than hers. If he only realized his ocean carried the same heart as the one splashing against a Carolina shore.

"Power's not for everyone," she said. "At least not for those who seek it."

He grabbed his chest, chuckling. "What dead poet did you steal that one from?"

"I don't know any dead poets, but I do like Chinese food."

He covered his face, letting out a wheezy laugh. "I'm starting to love these little chats."

The driver's fact-filled spiel sounded over the shuttle's intercom on top of the roaring engine. Everyone peered through the windows but them.

"Then why don't we just leave it between you and me." The limb she'd crept out on started to bow. "No more Mitchell."

His smile went standard, posed for a picture no one

was taking. "Is there a fortune cookie about fear in that pretty little head of yours?"

She pressed against the ice-cold metal beneath the window.

"I didn't think so." He scooted closer. "So, here's one: those who fear, survive. If you're going to survive, I have to keep Mitchell around because you're not as afraid of me as you should be."

She hugged herself, back pressing into the seat with as much force as her feet pressing into the floor. The FBI in her back pocket fueled her confidence and left her a little more brazen than she should be. Had he picked up on it?

"I'm scared enough to lie for you." She looked up at him, losing everything Forrest said she would. Even if it was only temporary, it was a feeling she would never forget.

His practiced face eased into something soft and distant. "Then November should come easy for you." He pointed outside as the shuttle reached a plateau. "We're here."

She unzipped her jacket and removed the lavender-scented candle.

"That'll never light out here," he said and moved into the aisle.

Patience waited for the shuttle to empty before she stepped into the blistering wind. Snowy footprints caught her boots as she trekked down the crowd's trail to a track of rocks and pebbles wrapping around the shore. She didn't miss the give of white sand nor the edges of a million broken shells. Not when the sea called with the echo of an endless hush.

"Home," she whispered into the wind. "This is what home feels like."

Frozen waves lined the surf, grabbing at the subzero air as ice patches floated across the ocean's surface. She drifted away from the group under the hazy sky to a bend in the shore beside a swirl of freezing sea water.

Back to the wind, she cleared a circle of the earth's gravel and placed the candle inside of it. She removed her glove, dug out her brother's lighter from her pocket and said a little prayer.

But the spark and the butane just wouldn't kiss.

The gusts changed direction again as Ana knelt before her, hands forming around the top of the candle.

Then Stiller came.

Then Paul.

The air stole Patience's tears. "Just a couple seconds. I only need a couple of seconds."

Trooper Andrews squeezed into their kneeling circle. He threw his coat over top their hunched bodies, closing their human dome.

She struck the spark wheel, her thumb raw.

The flame caught. Then the wick.

"Hey, Mom." She grinned. "I made it."

The last week of October arrived in a storm of over-caffeinated beverages, sleep deprivation, and paranoia. Mitchell showed his face enough to scare Patience into complacency. She'd only had to alter her data twice to keep it on track and show Governor Camden what he called *good faith*.

There was no word from Forrest, only praise from

Agent Martinez, support from Paul, and guidance from Ana who had the audio evidence to clear Forrest's name when the time came. Knowing she was doing the right thing and listening to people tell her it was the right thing, didn't make it any easier. Forrest needed to know, she wanted him to know, but it wasn't going to fix them.

"What are you going to do when this is all over?"

She coiled up in a squishy chair in the game room, incapable of looking Trooper Andrews in his baby blues. He'd been good to the team. "I don't know."

"I'm asking because I have a buddy back home who's struggling with something he says he didn't do."

"He's lucky to have you." Patience tucked her legs into her chest. "Have you known your buddy for a long time?"

"Longer than you."

"Then you know it's his way or the highway." She yawned.

"He's stubborn."

"Stubborn almost got him killed." She fought her heavy eyelids.

"What did you say?"

Patience blinked. Trooper Andrews leaned over and swatted her leg. "Wake up. What'd you say about Forrest getting killed?"

She pushed her hair out of her face. "Leave it alone, Dawson."

"Do you think this is funny?"

"You baiting me into confrontations every chance you get?" She glared at him. "Yeah. It's hilarious."

"His badge is on the line because of you."

"Harassing a victim might get your badge on the line

too."

He raised his fist to his mouth and squeezed his eyes shut. "You're a piece of work, you know that?"

"I don't have much of a choice since no one will listen to me."

"I've been trying to listen to you since I got here, but you won't say anything."

"I already told you everything is going to be all right."

"What if I don't believe that?"

"Then you'd be just like Forrest."

Trooper Andrews leaned back.

The snakiest of Camden's aides, Bobby, entered the game room. Patience checked her watch. "I'm going to wash up before dinner."

"I'll walk you."

"I'm good."

"I don't mind."

"Fine."

They walked the halls—Patience a prisoner to Dawson's allegiance, and he a prisoner to her silence. Every step took her closer to November, though, to a time beyond this moment where she visualized herself happy, safe, and free.

Dawson glanced around her empty room and left satisfied. She rested her forehead against the door. One more time she had to listen to Mitchell's voice. See him. Smell him. The bathroom door creaked open, and she rolled her head toward it.

You can do this. Ana's listening. You're going to be okay.

Governor Camden stepped into the room, a Cheshire-cat-smile stretching across his face. He held a silver, gift-wrapped box.

Holy shit. Jackpot.

"Governor Camden." A jittery fire lit beneath her. "I wasn't expecting you."

"I gave Mitchell the night off." He raised the present. "I have a little something for you. I wanted to give it to you in person."

His presence alone was all she needed. Every piece of audio Ana had collected, had been between Patience and Mitchell, enough to implicate the governor, but this—this turned the cat into the mouse.

"Is Mitchell still in Deadhorse?"

His head tilted slightly to the side, amber eyes darker than usual. "He's on his way to Fairbanks."

She fanned her fears down enough to speak. "You sent him after Forrest? Even though I've done everything you asked of me."

"Insurance, Pay." He extended the shiny, foil-covered box. "Open it. I think you'll like it."

"The survey is nearly over." She blinked away tears, trying to keep the conversation going. "What about my insurance? I altered the data. I'm giving you what you want. What if you kill Forrest anyways?"

He sighed and pulled on the tulle, glitter ribbon. "You've done decent work for me here. I'm not looking to damage our relationship. I'm just keeping it intact."

There was no relationship, just an invisible tether that had to be severed.

"I'm going to hand over the culmination of five months of fraudulent data in a matter of days." She swallowed. "I need to know he's going to be okay."

He came closer, tan leather dress boots not making

a sound as he glided passed the bed. "Are all the other MMO's okay? Their families? Their loved ones?"

"Corey." She shuddered.

"Corey controlled his fate as much as you do now." He rested a hand on her upper arm, thumb rubbing her shoulder. "Your colleagues are better off. In the long run, your whales might be too."

Plot points representing the truth of the Beaufort Sea hung on the wall behind him. "You promised me my own survey," she said. "You won't interfere again?"

He smirked. "The next one is all yours."

She nodded and took the box from under his arm. "What you'd get me?"

He tore the loose ribbon away. "Let's just say I made sure to get the matching clutch."

20

Tequila

Ana landed the Twin Otter on the runway at Fairbanks International Airport smoother than a kiss. Sun poured over the city in celebration of their escape from Deadhorse, bright for a late October day, but bone chilling-gusty, nonetheless. They unloaded on the tarmac, a white trooper SUV on one side of the plane and a black, heavily tinted SUV fifty yards behind it.

Ana had achieved her goal. She'd uncovered crimes, gathered evidence, and protected witnesses. Now all she had to do was get their C.I. out of there.

"I'll get her taxied," Paul said, wrapping Ana in a half hug.

She patted the side of the plane. "Thanks for taking care of my baby."

"Group hug," Stiller said. He pushed Patience into their arms, and they squeezed each other. Ana peeled herself out of the embrace. "Be good, city boy."

"Impossible," he said. "Where are you guys going again?"

Ana glared at Dawson loading the trooper SUV. Captain Thompson stepped out of the driver's side. "Girls weekend," she said.

Patience slung a duffle bag over her shoulder. "I'll see you when I get back to Anchorage, Stiller."

Luggage rolling behind them, Ana ushered Patience past Dawson and the captain. Agent Martinez appeared from the dark SUV in her signature gray pantsuit and opened the hatch.

"Associate of yours?" Dawson called at their backs.

"Uber." Ana smiled over her shoulder.

"Their clearance level is high these days," he shouted.

Grace stepped on the foot rail at the driver's side door and flipped her badge open, holding it in the air. "Thanks for the escort, Andrews."

"Damn it," Captain Thompson yelled.

Dawson threw his cap. "I fucking knew it."

"We'll be in touch." Grace jumped in the driver seat.

Ana climbed into the back behind Patience. The Tahoe tore off the tarmac as they buckled their seat belts. They'd survived Deadhorse.

Patience dug her phone out of her backpack. "I'm calling Dawson."

The car skidded to a halt. "Like hell you are," Grace said, high ponytail whipping around.

Ana put her hands up between them. "Can we please get out of here first? The best we know; Mitchell's already in Fairbanks."

"Dawson needs to know the truth about Forrest," Patience said.

Grace held her palm out. "Give me the phone."

Patience grabbed the door handle, tears welling up in her bloodshot eyes. "I'm making this call."

"Grace, we already messed with one troopers' life." Ana rubbed her chest, heart pounding.

Ana's sleep didn't go far into the night anymore. Too many moments she'd facilitated reeled through her mind. Could she use people like this forever?

Grace tossed her aviator sunglasses into the passenger seat. "*We* didn't do anything. Both of you made decisions in Deadhorse to achieve something. You were successful. We're moving on. The bureau will handle any residual effects."

"What's he going to do?" Ana asked. "Arrest her? They know we're with the FBI now. They know Forrest was right."

Grace sighed. "The damage is already done."

An undercover operative, Ana would remain nameless in all legal documents pertaining to the investigation into Governor Camden and Locke Industries. A ghost, really. Patience as well for her own safety. The troopers would be front-page news.

Ana wrapped her fingers around Patience's with a gentle squeeze. Patience squeezed back.

"I begged you to save Forrest," she said, voice breaking. "You wouldn't."

Ana's throat closed up. She had the audio to prove it.

Grace's fervor died as she slid her sunglasses back on and turned around in her seat. She removed her own phone from her coat pocket, scrolled through the screen, and then turned the speaker on.

Dawson answered, "Trooper Andrews."

Grace glanced over her shoulder at Pay and nodded. "It's Patience." Her shoulders rose as she inhaled.

"What do you want?" he asked.

"Well, you're the arresting officer."

Ana rubbed Patience's back, stare locked with Grace's in the rearview mirror.

"Let me put you on speakerphone so the captain can hear this," he said. "Go ahead."

Patience's head fell. "He didn't put his hands on me."

"I need you to meet me at the station," Dawson said.

"I can't," Patience whispered.

"Ms. Cline," Captain Thompson said. "You made accusations against a state trooper. There's a lot more to dropping these charges than a phone call."

Patience wiped her nose. "It's the best I can do right now."

"Forrest needs you to do this," Dawson said.

Ana's stomach twisted. Her friend had hurt someone to help them. She'd done the opposite. Face to face had tasted much different than locking in on a target ten thousand feet up and pressing a button. Logan's tattoos flashed in her mind close enough to touch. The arrows not pointing up or down, but in.

"I owe him more than a phone call," Patience said. "I know that, but it's all I got. I knew you needed to hear the truth, Dawson. I'll talk to you soon."

"Patience, wait—"

Grace ended the call. "We're done with the troopers from now on, ladies."

Isolation grew louder with every passing day, sweeping

Forrest's thoughts through a panoramic view of his life. It had been a month since he left Deadhorse. A month since he put on a uniform.

A month since he'd seen Patience.

The hard, frozen ground pressed against his sprawled-out body, keeping him level and steady. He settled his head behind the scope and pulled the trigger. A tree branch exploded at its base, tumbling down to the ground in a spray of fresh powder. Then another. Then another.

"Forrest?" Dawson came around the side of the cabin.

He climbed to his feet, hesitant to leave his one-man battleground, and removed his glove. "Trooper Andrews."

Dawson shook his hand. "Trooper Locke."

Not anymore.

"No Shave November, huh?"

A full, thick beard hid most of Forrest's face. Dark hair swirled beneath his black beanie and over his ears.

"If that's what you want to call it." He led Dawson up to the back porch, the sun setting at their backs in an orange glow.

"How are you holding up out here?"

Forrest studied the wooden planks beneath their feet for a moment then held the door open.

He wasn't holding up, not by his definition anyways. "Come on in."

Dawson stepped into a home Forrest kept immaculate. In the back of his pathetic mind, he hoped she might actually show up one day.

"Are you expecting someone?" Dawson pulled a hat

off his cropped, dirty blond hair. "I'm sorry I showed up like this. Your phone's been going to voicemail for a couple of days."

Forrest went to the kitchen and ducked his head into the fridge. "Want a beer?"

"Sure."

Evasion would only last so long, but Forrest didn't know if he could talk about it. Didn't know if he could get through a conversation about the weather without breaking down.

Dawson took the can and popped the tab. "You know I'm shit for small talk."

Forrest sat at his handcrafted kitchen table. Like most of the furniture in the cabin, he and Logan had made it together. He ran his finger along a rivet in the wood.

Dawson piled his hat and gloves on the table and sat on the matching bench seat. "The day I came back from Deadhorse with the MMO team..."

Forrest held his breath.

"Patience told us you didn't touch her."

Forrest wrestled his layers off to a red plaid flannel shirt and buried his face in his hands. He convinced his shoulders to heave in a long-winded rhythm, concentrating hard to distract his eyes from watering. This was coming. He knew that.

"Joe didn't want to tell you until he could give you your badge back, but Patience refused to come to the station to drop the charges. We both gave statements to the DA's office and they pulled my phone records. Forrest?" Dawson continued after Forrest lifted his head. "The moment she got away from me in Fairbanks, she called. I spent almost two weeks trying to get something out of her."

Forrest tried to think, but only scratchy words came out. "Where are you going with this?"

"She felt safe after we left."

He slapped his palms against the table in a rush of anger. "Because she got away from Camden. Away from Mitchell Wilson, the man who assaulted her."

She forced him out of the danger and subjected herself to it all, but why? Fear-tainted money?

"An FBI agent picked her and Ana up right on the tarmac." Dawson's jaw twitched. "Joe won't say for certain, but we've stopped pursuing any leads. I think we're taking a back seat."

"Someone hijacked our investigation, and she left me out to dry. Just like Logan." Forrest had gotten the troopers close enough to feel the mist of the storm brewing in the North Slope, and now they had nothing.

Dawson cleared his throat. "What happened with Logan?"

Forrest muffled delirious laughter. "My dad lawyered him up. They're saying he forced Mitchell Wilson's release from the Barrow jail because it was unlawful, based on an intimidated witness' statement, and I used excessive force in the arrest."

Dawson rubbed his eyes. "Damn, man."

"He stole Ana's room key. He gave Patience to Mitchell." Forrest shot up from the table before he put his fist through it. "I'm a goddamn scapegoat."

Dawson took a long swig of his beer, following Forrest to the kitchen. "There's one person who can refute all that."

Forrest palmed an unopened bottle of tequila on the counter. "And where is she?"

"I don't know. I can't find her." Dawson tossed the empty can into the trash.

"Exactly."

"I know this might be hard to hear." Dawson put a hand on Forrest's shoulder. "But she kept telling me everything would be all right in Deadhorse. I don't know how many times she said it."

"She ruined my life," Forrest whispered. Absence consumed him, whether it was the loss of her or his old life, it didn't matter."

"No. She left you."

He rubbed at the pain in his chest. "She gave me an ultimatum."

Dawson took the glass bottle of tequila, twisted the lid, and stared down into the clear liquid. "Still think you made the right choice?"

Emotion lodged in his throat. "Really?"

Dawson sipped the liquor, his face twisting as he put the bottle down. "Yeah, really."

Forrest wallowed near the bottom, knowing all too well he was his own anchor. "Came all the way here to ask me that?"

"I already know the answer." He took another sour-faced sip. "Because we both know you don't drink tequila."

ᐱ

Patience sealed her hand over her nose and mouth, nausea reigning control over her body at her father's office in Sunset Beach. The FBI had come to ask the same questions over and over again, sparring with her father's lawyers and infuriating Brenda to no end. Thanksgiving had come and gone. It was time to move on. They'd been wrong about Forrest.

"I'm going to be sick," she whispered.

Citrus cleaner assaulted her senses as an agent wiped a dry erase board clean. Since returning home, she'd been ill. Exhausted, but unable to sleep. A dry heaving ball of nerves. Brenda sat down with a can of 7UP and gently pressed the back of her hand to Patience's forehead.

"How long has it been since you've held something down?"

"A few days." Patience shrugged, heaviness dragging her shoulders down. "I don't think I can do this anymore."

Brenda turned to the muttering suits at the end of the table. "We're done."

Brenda's gentle grip led Patience out of her father's office. The bright and warm—by Alaska's standards—North Carolina air met them in the parking lot as they climbed into Brenda's Mercedes.

Breaks of light flashed against Patience's closed eyelids as she drove them away. She coiled into herself, heartache and victory too much for her system to handle.

"I think I'm going to die."

Brenda patted her knee. "Your father's cutting his fishing trip short. He's going to meet us at the hospital."

"Kidding." She gripped her knees tighter. "I was just kidding."

"You could use some fluids, and maybe they can help you get some sleep. You've been through a lot, sweetie."

No, this is just what happens when a man rips your heart out and spikes it on the frozen ground.

"It's only just starting, Brenda. I don't know how much more I can handle." She swallowed the emotion in her throat. "When's it going to get better? After the trial? How long is that going to take?"

Brenda lowered the radio volume. "There are things out of your control, and you need to understand that."

"That's the thing," she sniffled. "I was in control."

"But Forrest wasn't. When this is all over," Brenda grimaced and turned on the blinker, "months, years might pass. I just want you to be prepared for the worst."

Patience hugged herself tighter. "You're saying he might not forgive me."

Brenda pulled on her earing. "Men are different, Pay. How we're strong on the inside, they're strong on the outside and vice versa."

"This is going to sound awful," Patience said. "But I just want to be weak all over."

Brenda smiled. "If your mom could hear you now."

"You know you meant a lot to her, don't you?" Her eyes watered.

"Whenever I think I don't live up to her." The older woman grabbed Patience's hand and squeezed. "I think about you."

"I do the same thing." Patience closed her eyes, inhaling a deep breath. "Because I know you'll be there, no matter how many times I fuck up."

Brenda smacked her hand. "Language."

"Sorry," she smirked.

〢

Patience awoke to incessant beeping. Dim lights shone from behind the hospital bed, night peeked through the window, and the television murmured.

A young nurse in light pink scrubs slipped into the room and smiled softly. She followed the cord hiding beneath Patience's blanket then reattached the clamp to her finger. "These things never like to stay on. I'm Megan. I'll be taking care of you tonight."

Megan checked the IV line going into Patience's hand, ran a thermometer from temple to temple then adjusted the blood pressure cuff wrapped around her arm. "I'll have a light meal brought up to the room. Okay?"

"Sure, thank you." Patience reached for a tall thermos with a bendy straw. "How long do you think I'm going to be here?"

"Maybe another day. Maybe not. Dr. Lansing will be coming in soon to speak to you. Your father is asleep in the waiting room. Do you want me to get him?"

"No, no." Cold water poured down her throat. "Is Brenda here?"

Megan patted Patience's foot beneath the covers. "I'll check."

Patience sunk back into the bed rested but still tired. The clock on the wall said four-thirty in the morning. Days would turn into weeks, and then it wouldn't be long until she returned to Alaska, and maybe the thought of it was what was making her so sick—facing her decisions and their consequences.

She pulled the paisley print bag off the tray beside her bed and fished out her cell phone and a hair tie.

No calls.

Light crossed the dark room and a small woman in a white coat, wedge heels, and shoulder-length brown hair came in. "Hi, Patience. I'm Dr. Lansing. How are you feeling?"

Lonely. "Fine."

"Has the nausea subsided some?"

Patience nodded. "A little. It's pretty constant, though."

"I think I know what's going on, Patience. In your chart, I saw you use a patch for birth control?"

"Yes?"

"You switched from the pill about two months ago?"

"Yes." Patience balled the end of the sheet up in her hands. "I was doing research in the Arctic Circle and didn't want to worry about taking a pill every day."

"Was there a lapse in coverage?"

"Maybe a week."

Of course, the stupid patch was making her sick. Hormone overload from the fallout with Forrest. No wonder she had menstrual cramps and no actual period last month. Back on the pill she would go, and just maybe, she'd go a few hours without crying.

"It's good to use a backup for a couple of weeks when starting new birth control." She smiled. "I'm going to lean you back."

Megan rolled in a machine with a keyboard and a small screen. She lifted Patience's gown slightly above her hips and placed a white paper-towel-like square along the tops of her thighs.

"Hold on." Patience heart had missed a beat. "Why..."

She wrapped both hands around her mouth and squeezed her eyes shut. No, no, no, no, no.

Dr. Lansing grabbed a squirt bottle and a wand with a rounded end from the machine. "Your blood work—"

"No." Patience choked out a sob. "I can't."

"Relax." Dr. Lansing placed a hand on her shoulder. "We're just going to take a look, okay? Let's see what's going on before we jump to conclusions."

Cool gel hit Patience's skin, her head fell back, and pressure moved across her lower abdomen. The black screen on the ultrasound came alive with static gray.

"Left ovary looks good." Dr. Lansing tapped on the ultrasound machine's keyboard and drifted to the other side. "Right ovary looks good."

Images printed from the machine.

Patience stopped breathing as a sea of nothingness filled the screen. She wasn't mother material. She was just barely taking care of herself. Dr. Lansing pressed harder on the wand, angling it until a small, imperfect oval appeared in the darkness.

A white, digital plus sign appeared at the end of the oval then traversed to the other side. "Fetal pole," Dr. Lansing said quietly. "Yolk sac," she said of the shadow behind it. The white plus sign appeared again at the edge of the darkness, leaving a white dotted line behind as it crossed to the other side. "Six weeks, five days."

Brenda opened the door, a hopeful smile on her face and rushed to the bedside. "I have good news, Pay. The FBI cleared Forrest and—oh my God."

Patience couldn't look away from the screen. A baby. Forrest's baby.

Dr. Lansing printed a strip of images. "Acute morning sickness. It should subside by the second trimester. We'll get you hydrated, send you home with something for nausea, and have you follow up with your OB/GYN. Okay?"

Patience took the two images Dr. Lansing offered, astonished with tears falling down her face.

Brenda squealed. "We're having a *baby*?"

21

The Badge

Patience wandered around the safe-house in Fairbanks, hand hovering above the little, nine-weeks-along baby bump. They'd said she could see Forrest. They'd promised.

"I've been holding up my end of the deal since the beginning." She paced by Agent Martinez. "You haven't held up shit."

There'd been no rush to address the things Patience cared about, no perk to being a CI.

Grace's honey-brown eyes looked up at Patience. "I told you these things take time."

Patience adjusted a crooked picture hanging in the kitchen. "Too much time. I'll walk, Grace. I will."

Agent Martinez's heels clicked against the tile floor, stopping beside Patience. "You didn't come all this way for nothing."

She'd tried to do what was right. Tried to make a

difference. "It's not my fault Forrest wasn't your man."

"You're right. It's not. But you helped us get the men responsible."

"So why are we being punished?" Patience turned to the woman who had been her guide, her connection, her confidant. Worst-case scenarios squeezed by panic unraveled in her brain. "Why can't I see, Forrest? What's happened to him?"

Grace steadied Patience, the words she needed to hear not coming out.

"I'm done." Patience darted for the front door.

Grace beat her there. The bitch was fast in her heels. "Stop," she said.

"No." Tremors radiated out from Patience's chest. She needed to see Forrest. "Unless you're in the business of holding pregnant women hostage, get out of my way."

Grace stared at her abdomen and shook her head. "That's what's wrong with you."

"Wrong with me?" Patience demanded.

"Bad choice of words." Grace kept her hand on the door. "Listen, a hearing is being arraigned for Forrest. They'll drop his charges. You'll plead guilty to filing a false police report."

Her heart shot to her throat. "I get to be there?"

Every day he faced charges, every day he couldn't do what he was born to do, wicked away at her resolution. Everything was supposed to be okay but okay was so far away.

"No." Grace pinched her mouth shut. "That's why I didn't want to tell you."

Patience would not bend to the uncontrollable urge to cry. "I could have told him everything."

"Every decision he made in Deadhorse would have been compromised. It would have looked like a corrupt trooper covering his ass." Grace's tone elevated to new levels. "He was Camden's scapegoat. Locke Industries' scapegoat. You stopped that from happening."

Her eyes burned. "And he doesn't even know."

Grace held her fist to her forehead, eyes closed in thought. "The bureau will have my ass for this."

"I'm pregnant with his child, Grace," she pleaded. "I don't want to do this without him."

"Okay. Fine. Get ready."

⅄

Logan's truck wobbled down the uneven path to Forrest's cabin. He'd set out on an epic bender the night before but couldn't get one beer down. There was nothing to hide behind anymore. No crutch. No habit.

Locke Industries could suck it. They couldn't give him what he needed. Only he could do that.

Logan pulled his red Silverado, a truck nearly identical to Forrest's, down the empty gravel driveway. He'd wanted to be like his cousin in every way. It had taken a long time to realize he didn't have to be.

He jogged through the fresh powder, dusk letting the cold find its lung-burning, jagged edge. The quiet cabin he'd called home many of times opened with the same old key and welcomed him with the curtains open, thirsty for the light dying across the living room floor.

A chuckle slipped through his lips as he looked around, and walked to the fireplace, memories flooding his mind. If Forrest was here, he'd be trying to convince him to fight for the ridged, palm-sized metal in his hand.

Water filled his eyes and he took a deep breath. The firearm on his hip would go to Captain Thompson next, but he wanted to leave the badge with Forrest.

Floorboards creaked behind Logan followed by a muffled pop. He stumbled before he could turn, grabbing the edge of the fireplace mantle. Pain seared around his rib cage, a sharp breath scorched up his throat, and bricks met his knees.

"No..." Reality tilted like a sinking ship as he reached for the floor.

Logan grasped for his cell phone in his front right pocket, focus pulling from the direction the silenced shot came from to the knock at the front door. Patience peered through the window from the porch.

"No," he gasped. "No."

Her eyes met his and the heavy wooden door swung open. Another muffled pop. Her blonde hair flew in a twist and she fell.

Pain blossomed in his chest. Two loud bangs seared the air.

A woman with a dark ponytail knelt beside Patience, phone to her ear and weapon drawn. "Pay. *Pay.*"

This wasn't supposed to happen. They said nobody would get hurt.

This is all my fault.

Patience groaned and sat up slowly, palm pressed to her temple. "I'm okay. I'm okay."

"Officer down—gunshot wound to the back, civilian with injuries," the woman yelled into the phone. "Mitchell Wilson is traveling west on foot with a gunshot wound to the right shoulder, armed."

"I'm sorry." Logan wheezed. "I'm sorry."

"Stay with him." The woman ran to the back door. "Put pressure on the bleeding. Backup units are coming."

Patience crawled over, eyes widening the closer she got. "Oh my God, Logan."

Warmth poured down his back as he lay on his side. "First aid kit. Pantry."

Moments came and went. Patience packed his wound with gauze, her voice fleeting with his vision.

"Logan, stay with me."

I'm here, Pay. I'm here.

"Come on," she begged.

I'm here—it's just dark. I'm in the dark.

A force struck his chest. Then again. The familiar succession wasn't lost to him, but he was lost to the world. He'd give anything just to come back—just to place that badge in Forrest's hand.

Undisturbed, snow-covered, Forrest's backwoods country road—a quiet drive he wouldn't rush for anything, even if an avalanche roared behind him. Winter had settled in, coating his dazed life of grocery store trips and lawyer meetings. There was nowhere to be and no one to see.

Logan's Truck and a black SUV appeared around the bend. He eased to a stop in front of his mailbox. The front door was open. Muscle memory took over as he exited his vehicle, sirens blaring in the distance. Weapon drawn, he snuck alongside the empty cars, heart hammering in a way it hadn't in a long time.

What happened?

He crept onto the porch, and there Patience was

beyond the threshold, in his living room, hunched over Logan's lifeless body in the midst of compressions. Blood dripped from a stream pouring down the side of her face.

"One, two, three," she murmured, "four, five, six, seven, eight."

A badge lay in a crimson puddle bleeding into the knees of Patience's jeans. A bullet graze scored her left temple. The people he loved.

In a crime scene.

"It was Mitchell." Her lips mouthed the count of a life-saving rhythm. "Grace went after him."

Bloody footprints led toward the back door. Helicopter blades beat the air overhead.

"She's FBI." A terrified, gut-wrenching look crossed Patience's face. "Stay with me. Please."

The disconnect that had become Forrest's shadow pulled ahead, cutting through the fog of emotions he couldn't bear to feel.

There was only one side and one thing to do.

He backed away, consuming his own silent hell and turning it into purposeful energy. First responders swarmed the cabin. A paramedic pulled Patience away from Logan and took her to the entryway bench. He couldn't listen to her hysterical gasps, couldn't fathom this moment lasting one second longer.

He took a knee in front of her, refusing to be a victim—to be hurt. "I have to go."

"No." Tears streaked through the red smear on her cheek.

"I have to stop him." The key to his gun cabinet met his fingertips.

"What if he stops you?" Her frightened, glassy eyes struck him dead in the chest.

He shoved the doubt away. "He won't. Nobody knows these woods like I do."

This was his territory. His land. It had all come back to him to finish, just like it should.

"Forrest." She raised her shaky hand to Logan being rolled onto a body board. "Who do you think Mitchell came here for?"

What did it matter? The whys, the reason—none of it changed the outcome. None of it changed the past. Mitchell had to be caught. It was Forrest's responsibility.

It was his fault.

Patience's question stabbed at his brain, reaching for the fragile places he guarded, threading that connection he so desperately needed to be severed.

Logan had come to his house, in a truck just like his, looking just like him—like he always had since they were children. Forrest caught the ground before it caught him, and he sat on the floorboards.

Did Mitchell come for him? Was that bullet his?

The paramedic coached Patience into deep breaths as troopers scattered evidence markers around his living room. A man in a suit gave direction in between phone calls as Logan's half-dead body passed by.

Dawson squatted down in front of Forrest. "Hey, man. You all right?"

The badge glimmered on the ground behind Dawson, fallen, just like his cousin. Why'd he come here? After everything he'd done, why'd he come back?

"Forrest?" Dawson tapped his shoulder.

"Yeah?" he asked.

"Are you okay?"

No. He wasn't. Nothing was okay.

"Listen." Dawson grabbed Forrest's coat. "This is the FBI's investigation, but I thought you should know." He paused, eyes drifting to the pool of blood, and sucked in a deep breath. "Logan called the captain when he got here. Said he had to make things right with you, and he'd be coming to the station to turn himself in."

Forrest pulled himself up onto the bench beside Patience, an avalanche of fear pouring over his shoulders, breaking and burying him up to his neck.

"LifeMed is flying him to a trauma center." He squeezed Forrest's shoulder. "We're going to get that son of a bitch. You hear me?"

Forrest nodded. A bullet wasn't the only thing someone had been trying to give him today—but an apology too. And he would have accepted it.

He reached blindly for Patience, ignoring the paramedic's objection until she was in his lap and cradled in his arms. Something warm to hold against all his cold. Something he cared about.

Some hope.

"Why are you here?" Welled up tears fell, running into his beard.

"Same reason Logan was." She choked out the words.

He put his lips to her caked hair, eyes pinned shut to hide what would still be there when he opened them.

She shivered. "To fix everything."

Paramedics tried to pry Patience away, but the more she cried, the more he cried. It hurt to let them take her, so much so that he fought to keep her. He couldn't lose her all over again. He couldn't lose anymore.

"She's got a head wound." His captain's voice begged him for reason. "She needs to go to the emergency room."

Forrest was beyond reason. There was no protocol for this. No procedure to follow. These were the people he loved.

Captain Thompson and Dawson pinned his elbows. A paramedic slid Patience's arms from around his neck.

"I love you." Her pained smile shattered his false sense of reality.

What had he done? How did they get to this place?

"I love you, too," he croaked.

Dawson muscled him away from the foyer in a stumbling haze. The man in the suit pointed for them to go to Forrest's bedroom. Heavy feet dragged him passed the bullet hole in his kitchen to a striking Latina woman in her mid-thirties, pacing in a gray pantsuit.

"I've seen you before." Dawson sent Forrest a warning glance.

"Shut the door behind you, Trooper Andrews." Daggers in her eyes somersaulted across the room.

Dawson held his ground until Forrest nodded, leaving with one final look over his shoulder.

The stranger offered her hand. "Agent Grace Martinez, FBI."

"Forrest Locke." I *think*. This was his home. These were his things around him.

"You can accept our protection, Mr. Locke or the bureau can detain you indefinitely for questioning. It's your choice."

"Whoa, whoa," he stammered. "Did you get him?"

"I need an answer."

"I need answers," he shouted.

The law had taken a back burner to his pain—a first. He'd been in the dark too long. They'd swept not just his investigation from under him, but Patience too.

"I wounded him," she said. "We've got a good trail."

Forrest couldn't hold back. "The only good thing you have right now are Alaska State Troopers doing your job for you."

"Get in line or I will detain you." She reached for cuffs behind her back.

"You want my cooperation, you tell me what the fuck you're doing here."

"You want to know what's going on here?" Agent Martinez cocked her head to the side. "My CI almost took a bullet to the head is what's going on here."

"CI?" Patience was an informant?

"We reached out to Patience after you arrested Mitchell in Deadhorse. She agreed to help us."

If he'd listened to her, trusted her, he might have been around to protect her. All she'd asked was that he'd stick by her side. How blind had he been? How could he miss this?

"That's where she's been, with you?"

She nodded.

"Those allegations she made against me—you put her up to that?"

"No." She crossed her arms tightly. "She did that on her own."

Forrest leaned back on his dresser, trying to piece things together. The entire time he'd been on the outside.

"If details are your thing," Agent Martinez stared at the ground, "She took matters into her own hands when we denied her request to pull you out of Deadhorse. She felt your life was in immediate danger."

He shook his head. The danger had followed them home no matter how hard Patience had tried to stop it. "She was helping you, but you wouldn't help her? Is that what you're telling me?"

"That's becoming an unfortunate theme." Agent Martinez cleared her throat. "I explained to Patience that the FBI's investigation didn't stop at Governor Camden and Locke Industries, but at you, especially after we traced the ten thousand dollars back to your bank account."

His eyes burned. She'd known about the money but hadn't said a word, hadn't let it shake her faith in him. "It didn't stop her from doing what she thought was right, though."

"No. She got you out of Deadhorse and got us what we needed."

Acid crept up his neck. "Did they hurt her?"

"Not until she demanded to see you today." She covered her mouth, looking around at nothing. "I should have never brought her here."

Forrest kept his head above the guilt just enough to breathe.

"We know you had nothing to do with what happened in Deadhorse *now*." She smoothed her hair back. "I know you'd rather the troopers handle this, but I'm going to ask you to help us anyways."

Help. Now they wanted it.

"I need to get to Fairbanks Memorial to see my family. That's all I know."

Grace straightened her back. "I know this is difficult—"

"No, you don't know." He reached for the doorknob.

"I gave you your choices. You can tell your story in an interrogation room, or in an undisclosed, safe location."

He treated people this way—forcing their hand in situations only he could control. The unexpected insight didn't make it any easier for him to listen to what she had to say

"Or not at all," he said. "I know how this works. You've got to already have Patience in a protection program. I know where that leaves me, especially if this case goes to trial and we're sequestered. You're going to take her away from me, and I need to be with her as long as I can before you do."

"The FBI makes exceptions," she said. "Judges will make exceptions, especially to a hometown hero."

He let out a hard laugh. "Hero? That's what you're going to paint me as?"

"Forrest, listen to me."

"Listen to empty promises?" he asked.

She shook slightly, hands opening and closing at her sides. "If I tell you the FBI will make an exception for you and Patience in our witness protection program, I mean it."

"Bullshit."

"You've never made an exception for anyone?" she snapped.

Logan's words flooded the forefront of his mind. Forrest was always a straight shooter. A man who played by the book. A walking moral compass of his own discretion. Then Patience.

"It means too much to me to put it in someone else's hands," he whispered, life trying to leave his body on a breath.

"That is something I do understand." She stared at him—past the law, past the façade of an enforcer, to the kind of person who dedicated their lives to helping others no matter the personal sacrifice.

"If I agree to help you, what happens next?"

"We get Patience then I hand you both over to the U.S. Marshal Service while I clean up this mess."

He held the door open, but couldn't walk through. Patience had been compliant with the FBI. Did that mean he could be too?

Agent Martinez eased into his vision. "Let's start moving forward. Do our part because she's doing hers."

22

Promise

Fluorescent light splashed off the pale blue tile floor ahead of Patience's footsteps. Citrus with undertones of antiseptic laced the air all the way to her room in the emergency department. Her guard, a rigid clone of an FBI agent, had vacated his post to hover outside the commotion in the triage bay. Good. She could use the space.

Numbness spread from her core to her skin as she entered the small exam room, blanketing her in a moment that just wouldn't end. A bouquet of white lilies and white pine leaves sat beside the oozing hand sanitizer dispenser on the counter. A silver ribbon adorned the glass vase.

"Didn't want to come empty-handed." His voice hit her like a shovel, jolting her sad, quiet heart.

Governor Camden shut the door, never rising from the small black stool in the corner. Their relationship twisted like a soaked cloth, refusing to drip no matter how far she stretched it.

"How could you?" She grimaced.

A tender ache spread through her scalp as exhaustion filled her bones. Her protective shell cracked, leaving her cold in borrowed, baggy scrubs.

Strangely unkempt in his rumpled dress shirt and scuffed boots, he crossed his legs, locking swollen hands around his knee. "I had nothing to do with the attack on Forrest today."

A blood vessel split his forehead, no doubt feeding the tension in his face. Odder than the sweat on his brow was the look in his eye.

"I don't fuck up," he said at her silence.

Patience sat on the hospital bed, mesmerized by the concern in his stare. This wasn't the Camden she knew. "I don't believe you."

"I'm not the back-stabber in this relationship, Pay. That would be you." He cleared his throat.

In her own disloyalty and lies, she reeled in his. She balled up the side of her pant leg in her fist. Odds. She'd been at inescapable odds with him, with the FBI, with Forrest.

"You disappeared." He cocked his head to the side. "Like a witness in a protection program."

"You don't know what you're talking about," she snapped then smoothed the fabric on her thigh.

"We're both just trying to get the job done here. You're trying to save the whales," He waved his hand in the air like he was selling a painting she wasn't buying, "and I'm trying to get to a big white house."

"What I'm doing," she huffed, "is called surviving."

It wasn't just her and Forrest anymore. There was a baby coming into the world. That was not a life to play with. All the things she shouldn't have done, wouldn't have done, didn't matter anymore.

"I had nothing to do with what happened today." He flexed his pink hands then crossed his arms, tucking them away. "And you need to know that."

"It was Mitchell," she said. "I was there. I saw him. He tried to kill me."

He shook his head. "Not my orders."

A shot rang in Patience's ears over and over. "You're not going to forgive me and let me walk away from this. This was you."

He closed his eyes, sighing long and hard. "That's the thing, Pay. I do forgive you for going to the FBI. It probably saved your life. Your future in-laws, they're not forgiving like me."

Worry flashed through her as his eyes opened.

She swallowed. "You're saying they tried to kill their own son?"

"Yes. That puts us in a position to help each other." He nodded to himself.

"Help me?" she wondered aloud. "Why would you help me?"

"Because you helped me open the Beaufort Sea. Now you're going to help the FBI take down Locke Industries." His stare bore into hers.

She should have known he never had any intention of taking the fall. "Sounds like you're getting your cake and eating it too."

He managed his signature smile. "Wedding cake is my favorite. Maybe I can gift you one?"

"I don't want any more gifts." How could he think he still had any power over her? "I want you to close the Beaufort Sea for drilling."

"Pay, that's behind us." He chuckled.

"It's not behind me. You're going to clean up your oceans."

"And tell Locke Industries what?" He shrugged. "That some girl made me? You saw what they did to their own family. What do you think they'll do to me?"

"That's why you're going to help the FBI."

"No. Absolutely not." His head swiveled side to side. "I can't do that."

"I'll vouch for you," she offered. The man made deals and lived off of them. But it wouldn't be his terms this time.

He gawked at her, looking around at an absent audience. "I'll lose everything."

"You'll lose everything and more if you don't."

Deadhorse had forged a path they both traveled on, walking toward each other, but always knowing there was only one way to go.

Her way.

He stood, lips twitching to the side, and buttoned his sleeves at the wrists. "Shoot me a text if Mitchell's not dead-on-arrival, okay? I can't have anything more on the table than I already have."

Her heart thumped. "Wait, what are you talking about?"

"Who do you think he called to pick his bleeding ass up in the middle of the woods?"

"You," she murmured, a weight rising from her shoulders.

He pointed to the bandage on her head, taking in an uneasy breath. "They're scared of Forrest, and they jeopardized everything sending Mitchell after him, and Mitchell jeopardized me when he made that phone call."

She couldn't ignore his cry for justification, nor her relief. "So, you did what you had to do?"

"And it looks like I'm going to keep doing that. Tell Agent Martinez I'll be in touch."

He cracked the door, eyed the hallway for a few seconds, and then slipped out. Patience stared at the bouquet. Mitchell wouldn't be coming back for Forrest or for her.

But he'd been someone's puppet.

Voices sounded through the wall, growing louder with every minute, and then a code came over the hospital's intercom. After a light knock, the young FBI agent came in.

"A body showed up. It's beaten pretty badly," he said. "There's a bullet wound to the right shoulder. It might be our guy. Think you can try to I.D. him?"

She got to her feet. "I think I can."

人

Forrest led the way into the emergency department, trailed silently by Agent Martinez. His job brought him to this place too often. Familiar faces waved him through.

Dr. Ian Burroughs came around the nurse's station, I.D. flapping against his blue scrubs. "Sounds like it was a close one."

They exchanged a quick hug, Dr. Burroughs' hand lingering on Forrest's shoulder. They'd lost people in this emergency room before, but he wouldn't have the ones he cared about treated by anyone else.

"We got Logan to the OR." Ian ran a hand over his short, salt and pepper hair.

Forrest swallowed. "Should be me in that OR."

"You can't think like that." Ian sighed. "You know better."

Agent Martinez drifted back as emotion climbed up Forrest's throat. He'd never been so helpless before.

"Hell," he whispered, holding back the tears. "If Patience hadn't of shown up, he'd be in a body bag. A couple of inches to the right and she'd be too. Ian, I've never been through something like this before."

"I don't know what's going on," he whispered, stare reaching for Agent Martinez, "but I want you to look out for yourself. Dawson came in with Logan, and I know he's only been on the job for a little while, but he's really shaken up."

"Someone came after me—after a trooper." He swallowed. "They got Logan, but they were looking for me. It really should have been me."

"But that's not what happened." He grabbed Forrest's shoulders. "Logan might pull through, and I pray to God he does, and Patience is fine. Just an abrasion on her head. We did an ultrasound too just to be on the safe side and everything looks good. Strong heartbeat."

Forrest stared into his friend's hope-filled brown eyes. "Ultrasound? What are you talking about?"

Ian's mouth fell open. "You didn't know?"

They turned to Agent Martinez. She coughed, cleared her throat and pointed down the hall. "I need to find Agent Barnes."

A sea of trepidation swept at Forrest, surging like a tide in a hurricane. Patience was pregnant. He was going to be a father. The fear receded cautiously into the depths of his mind, leaving a shore of unknown possibilities, but the mistakes he'd made, the pain he'd caused, couldn't match his awestricken heart.

Fatherhood. His child. Their child.

"Ian?" he asked. "Really? You're sure?"

"She's almost ten weeks." He grinned. "Mom has been through a lot today."

Mom. Patience a mother. A swell of joy crested over the fear of what he could have lost today.

"Where is she?" he demanded.

"I'm right here."

Just the sight of Forrest unraveled Patience. Their life had begun the night of a Chicago thunderstorm, grounded together in other people's betrayal, their pain and a luxury suite. They'd found each other again in the Arctic—an inevitable fate Alaska was going to make happen no matter what—she was sure of it

Images of the past, present, and future reeled through her mind. She latched onto them with a fearless hope. They'd gotten this far and there didn't have to be a limit to how far they could go.

Everything faded into the background as he swarmed the space between them, his lips parting and pinching together. Watery eyes tried to say the things he couldn't. Wild, dark hair fell onto his forehead as he pulled his knitted cap off. She'd never seen his beard so thick before, or the look he gave her. So far removed from the trooper. So raw.

He knew.

"I'll take care of you and that baby for the rest of my life," he promised. "I swear."

Chills fell down her body, coiling passed the heat racing up it. This man would be her partner. She grabbed his face as he folded her into his arms, the green in his eyes blazing hotter than the palms at her back. Happy tears slipped between their lips, coating her tongue with a salty-sweetness.

For every mile that had separated them, she kissed him. It tasted better than the first time. A swirl of the familiar and the uncharted shot straight through her.

"Patience?"

She turned to Agent Martinez. "Yes?"

"Time to move out."

She blushed at their pink faces. "One more thing."

Forrest slid her down his body to the ground, and she gripped his arm in a haze, wiping away the wetness on her face with the back of her hand. A sideways smile lifted his cheek as he fixed her hair, tucking stray pieces behind her ears.

A strange peace wrapped around her. "Mitchell. He's dead."

The color drained from Forrest's face. "You're sure?"

"You should see for yourself."

Forrest wadded his hat up and followed Dr. Burroughs and Agent Barnes to the triage bay. He deserved to see for himself. No more doubt over the fate of the person who'd shot his cousin.

Agent Martinez nudged Patience. "You know anything about this?"

She turned just before the curtain opened. A dead body had been a first for her, but she'd needed to see it just like Forrest needed too.

"Depends. Are you ready to make another deal?" She had to get out of Fairbanks.

Grace sucked her bottom lip in. "He contacted you, didn't you?"

"He came here." Patience warded off the tremor moving down her spine.

Grace shook her head at the ground then scanned their surroundings. "This is why I didn't want you back in Alaska yet."

Patience looked back at Forrest. He shook Dr. Burroughs's hand and pulled his hat on, hiding his furrowed brow. "If what he told me is true, I need to get as far from Locke Industries as I can. Me and Forrest. Tonight."

"U.S. Marshalls are already on their way." She straightened as Forrest approached. "No more exceptions, Pay. We do this my way."

She swallowed. "Okay."

Forrest's hand slid into Patience's. "Where are we going?" he asked.

"The Marshall Service is taking you to a safe location, Forrest. Patience will be taken separately."

"No." His grip tightened. "Where she goes, I go."

"You're too dangerous for her to be around right now."

Patience kept her hand away from her stomach, the guilt on Forrest's face too much for her to stand. "I'll be there, Forrest. I swear."

"What if you're not?" His face reddened. "What if

something happens to you, and I'm not there again?"

"And what if someone else comes for you?" Her heart pounded. "I'm scared, too, but we can't do this on our own."

A clean-cut man in business casual attire entered quietly through the double doors behind them. The light caught his silver belt buckle.

"It's time, Forrest," Grace said.

"I don't know if I can do this." He pulled Patience aside, wrapping her in his massive arms.

She nestled into him, ear pressed against the thundering in his chest. "But we need you to."

He kissed the top of her head, shaking with breaths that only grew shorter and shorter. She eased back and stared into his tear-filled emerald eyes, hurting simply because he did.

"We'll come back to you," she promised. "There's nothing in this world that can stop me."

He lowered his lips to hers and kissed her softly. "I have so much to say to you."

"You'll get your chance." She smoothed a dark curl back under his hat.

Grace waved the Marshall over. "Take him by post-op then get him the hell out of here."

ᴧ

A cloud of morphine hovered over Logan's body and he fought it with every thread of his being. Twisted memories bled into nightmares. Forrest dead on the cabin floor. Ana and Patience too.

"Logan?"

He knew that voice. *Open your eyes.*

"I don't know if you can hear me," Forrest said.

I can. He tried to move, reach, touch. Pressure from the obliterated yellow buttercup on his back tried to swallow him.

"I just...I just wanted you to know." His voice broke. Logan had never heard Forrest cry before. Hot liquid seeped beneath his eyelids. "I know you've made some mistakes, but it should have been me. You didn't deserve this."

Tears streamed passed Logan's temples. He clung to consciousness, fighting the painless promise.

"You're my brother. Always have been." Forrest's strong grip wrapped around Logan's forearm.

He didn't know if he could listen. He didn't know how many forms of self-inflicted hurt he could handle.

"I love you," Forrest said. "I know you can be the man you want to be."

Logan's fingers moved, and he grasped Forrest's hand. The harder he squeezed the closer to oblivion he came. Grooved metal slid into his palm as he drifted away.

人

Ana's "interview" with the FBI ended the day everyone returned from Deadhorse. Agent Martinez took her gear and intel, promised to stay in touch, and had told her she'd done an excellent job. No one from the agency had contacted Ana since.

Per protocol, she was to have no contact with any persons involved in the investigation. Then Dawson called. She didn't have the answers to his questions, but she did have a Twin Otter and time.

Captain Thompson snuck her into the dark room. The FBI had left Logan to the troopers for the duration of his recovery. Ana figured that'd be his preference anyway.

Wires ran to the monitors on the sides of his bed. He breathed quietly on his own, splayed out on his back, hair a mess against a white pillow.

She sat in a beige pleather chair, a lump forming in her throat.

His eyes peeled open. "Ana?"

"Yeah." Her voice mimicked the strain in his. "It's me."

"What are you doing here?"

She blinked away the water in her eyes. "Nothing. I just love hospital food."

He grimaced and smiled. "Makes sense."

Cool skin met her palm as she rubbed his tattooed bicep. The delicate lines and the repeating pattern of pointy arrows were gone, replaced with a flood of black ink. "Does your other arm look like this?"

He nodded at the blood pressure cuff around his arm, and her heart tried to break, to shatter, but she wouldn't let it.

"Why?" she asked.

Raw, scratchy words came through his lips. "I didn't live up to it."

"Yes, you did."

She shrugged her jacket off then pulled her arm out of her long sleeve sweater. Soul searching after Deadhorse brought Ana full circle. Fate took her where she needed to be to show her where she came from. A replica of his tattoos wrapped around her forearm.

He turned his head away, face crumbling. "Leave."

Breath slipped from her lungs. "Logan..."

"Please, leave."

She slid her sleeve down, commanding herself not to break, and pulled her jacket on. "You may have gotten those tattoos first, but I think they were meant for me."

His breath hitched.

"I went home. An elder in my family did it." A monitor beeped and she stood, backing away. "Now I understand why he was so willing."

His body trembled, his gaze never leaving the wall. "Stay away."

She took her time with each button, despair trying to drown her, but she knew it would be this way. "If you need to see them again, find me."

"You wouldn't say that if you knew me." His chest heaved.

She tucked her scarf in. "I know you lost yourself in Deadhorse."

He faced her, pale and clammy, eyes bloodshot and desperate. "I lost myself a long time ago."

Tears streaked down her face as she fastened the last button. "You tried to leave my room. I should have let you go." She wiped her face. "I was madder at myself than you when you took that key."

"I'm sorry," he whispered. "I'm so sorry. I'd take some of it back, but I wouldn't take it all back."

She closed her eyes, the darkness pulling her back to that night.

"I'm not good for you." His voice ground the words into a murmur. "I wish to hell I was, but I'm not."

"I know." She wouldn't sob until she got outside. "I

knew this would be goodbye. I always knew it would be goodbye."

"Don't look back," he said. "Promise me you won't because I'm never going to do the right thing."

"I won't," she sniffled, angry at him, at herself, at everyone. "I'll leave the looking back to you, and if I never see you again, I'll be okay."

"I know you will." He closed his eyes. "Go. Please, go."

Ana didn't stop until she made it to the snow. It poured from the sky in an attempt to disguise the land as a mountain top, but she wouldn't be fooled. She'd trudge through it.

She had to.

23

Breaching

Patience rode shotgun, taking in the quaint coastal town along the South Carolina-Georgia border. The Marshalls placed them far from Alaska, in a place like the beach she grew up on. A bustling holiday crowd filled the ice cream parlors, gift shops, and niche restaurants. It was all so picturesque, but it wouldn't be right until she saw him, until she touched him. It had been three long days since she'd seen Forrest, and there was no postcard town worth visiting without him.

The sun began to set as Grace pulled the SUV beneath a pale-yellow house on stilts.

"This is home for now," she said.

"You didn't have to bring me all the way out here." Patience undid her seatbelt. "I know you have to go back to Alaska."

"I owed it to Forrest." She put her sunglasses on top of her head, her big brown eyes looking everywhere but where Patience sat. "You'll be here while we finish raiding Locke Industries, see if the hit on Forrest came from them."

Patience wrapped her arms around her belly. "And if it didn't?"

"Then the truth died with Mitchell Wilson."

Patience stared at the flip-flop welcome home sign hanging in the carport. "I don't think the governor sent him after Forrest."

"We don't know that for certain," Grace said. "But we do know Samuel Locke has fled the country."

"When?" Patience asked.

"The day of the shooting." She dropped her sunglasses back down to her face. "Forrest has been briefed on the situation. There's a lot you need to talk about."

She nodded, grabbing the door handle. "Maybe when this is all over, me, you, and Ana can go fly planes or shoot guns or do something I like."

She smirked. "I hear drunk painting is a thing. You know, when you're done being pregnant."

Patience reared back. "You? An artsy wine connoisseur?"

"Nah." She shook her head. "I'd rather drink scotch and melt crayons if I'm being honest."

Patience snorted.

"Get out of here." Grace rubbed her brow. "There's a Marshall waiting inside for you."

"Scotch and crayons." Patience chuckled and stepped out of the car. "Got it."

"Pay, one second." Grace reached across the front seat and stopped the door from closing. "I'm sorry we didn't nail Camden. Got a small victory for the whales, though."

The governor had come through in a masterful way, a way Patience once feared he'd use on Forrest. He gave the FBI Joseph Locke, and the powers-that-be kept him on track for the big white house. They'd been scapegoats for his choosing no matter the evidence piled against him. He was untouchable, like the Beaufort Sea, which he closed for offshore drilling.

"There's a lot more ocean left," Patience said.

Grace adjusted the rearview mirror. "Then you better get to work."

She smiled to herself. "Soon as you let me."

Patience searched the wicker-furniture filled home until she found a Marshall on the back balcony, sipping from a conch-shaped coffee mug. He pointed to the beach.

Dusk painted a blood orange hue across the shore, leaving the man in the surf a familiar shadow. Weathered boards met her bare feet one by one until she reached the black-streaked sand behind the dunes. Sea oats waved as she went into the days fading light, her heart fluttering like her cotton dress in the wind.

Forrest tossed shell after shell into the ocean, skipping the shards across the surface in a dark baseball cap, white T-shirt, and gray board shorts. Just as his name was about to leave her lips, he stilled, pieces falling from his fist into the sand at his feet.

Patience carried the fabric of her dress above the cool, giving Earth, searching for what he stared after in the sea. The water broke, and she held her breath.

A North Atlantic Right Whale lunged from the ocean, signaling a message for her migratory sisters—a message

Patience would spend her life trying to understand. She stood beside Forrest, his awe of the massive, splashing creature deepening her awe of him. The wonder and appreciation on his handsome face would stay with her forever, and one day, she'd get to share it with their child.

"Patience," he murmured. "If you could only see this."

"There's nothing like it," she said.

His gaze flashed to hers. An arm scooped around her waist as the beach tilted and they fell into the sand.

"I'm sorry." His stare dropped to her stomach as he lay her gently down. "Are you okay?"

"I'm fine." She ran the backs of her fingers along his clean-shaven face. "I've missed you so much."

Patience's days and nights had passed slowly after Deadhorse, stretching like the miles that had separated them, but they'd made it to the same coast once again.

He shoved her dress up to her navel.

"*Forrest.*"

Head down, he caressed the firm swell above her boy-short underwear. "I know you didn't plan on this."

She glanced around the lonely beach, pushed his cap off, and ran her fingers through his freshly cropped hair. "I cried. I was terrified."

Then the hole her mother left behind had become a tiny bit smaller.

"But it feels right, Forrest."

"I know it does." He sniffled. "You shouldn't have been going through this alone."

"You didn't know."

He looked up, the hurt shining through his vibrant eyes. "I should have never left you the way I did."

The past coiled up into a tight ball in her throat. "I didn't give you much of a choice."

He pressed his lips to her stretching skin. "You protected me, and I never thought I needed someone to do that."

She blinked away the tears. All the pain she'd caused him to protect him couldn't be erased. "But I cost you so much."

He folded her dress down and settled above her, shaking his head. "No."

The approaching tide morphed her fears into words. "I was coming back to Alaska to show you I wasn't the person you thought I was, even if you hated me."

"I'm not going to lie." His face softened. "I waited for you every day. I thought you sold me out like everybody else did, and I tried to be angry about it, but there was nothing I wanted more than for you to walk through my front door."

Forgiveness—something she hadn't been sure he could achieve, but would have asked him for, surfaced all on its own.

"I'm sorry for all the things I didn't say, Forrest." Tears slid down her temples. "I really am."

"And I'm sorry for the things I did say." His red-rimmed, bright green eyes never left hers. "I just want to be everything you need, everything our child needs."

"You will be."

She'd make sure of it.

Tears streamed down his cheeks, and he turned toward the ocean. "Oh shit."

∧

Forrest rolled to his side just in time for the tide to hit his back. Winter-chilled surf jolted his body, soaked his clothes, and ignited a series of curse words he couldn't rein in. Patience scrambled to her feet, laughing in a cove of untouched sand.

She grinned, a violet sky falling on her white dress like a dream he'd been chasing his entire life. Someone had tried to take it all away from him with a single shot. Ousted at Locke Industries, his father faced a decade's worth of federal indictments. Then there was Sam, guilty by association, but conveniently outside the country. If Camden had made the call to end Forrest's life, that secret died with Mitchell Wilson. It all left Forrest with one question to ask his angel on Earth.

He knelt, too stunned to stand. "I want you in my life every day. Whatever I have to do. Whatever it takes."

She chuckled and covered her mouth, gaze cutting straight to his soul.

"I mean it," he promised.

"I know you do." She smiled at her feet then up at him. "Let's get you out of those wet clothes."

He stood in the rays of the setting sun, and she backed away with every step he took. "Where do you think you're going?" he asked.

She squealed and dashed to the beach house, a trail to heaven flying behind her in the cool evening air. A few strides and she was cradled in his arms, soft hair blowing in his face. The sand turned to wood planks, the wood planks to ceramic tile, the tile to the azure rug beneath a four-post king-size bed.

He placed her on her feet just as her lips pressed to his, deliberate hands lifting his damp shirt. Chills covered his skin as he pulled it over his head, ball cap hitting the floor.

Straps fell over her shoulders with the guide of his hands, slipping past her bare chest, curved hips, and trembling legs. He lifted her from the circle of fabric around her ankles, warm breasts pressing into his cool skin as she slid her mouth over his neck. Every graze of her tongue on his flesh intensified the fire she'd started inside of him—a fire started that Chicago night. He ripped the covers back on the bed and placed her in the center, mesmerized by the tiny swell of their creation.

They were bound together in the most beautiful way he could think of.

She held her arms out to him, and the beckoning in her eyes had him peeling his board shorts off as quickly as he could muster.

"I'm coming, honey." He climbed onto the bed

She pulled his face up to hers, gaze full of ideas he'd spend the rest of his life exploring. The way she kissed him brought him to his elbows, and he cradled her head in his hands, lost in the welcome of her sweet lips.

He'd never been in control when it came to Patience. Whether he deserved the reward for such trust, he didn't know, but he would embrace the way it melted his nerves into a river of bliss coursing through his veins.

He dragged his lips down to her breast, her chest rising to meet his mouth as his palm slid south. A soft moan accompanied the swirl of his tongue around the hard peak, echoing louder with each pull of his lips.

Cotton hit his fingertips and his cock throbbed harder, the pressure of her hip far from enough. She slid her panties from under her ass and he dragged them up her legs before tossing them to the floor.

He drifted to the other breast, middle finger testing the hot folds between her legs and delving into the wetness.

He shifted his hips between her thighs, beyond ready to feel her all around him.

Fingernails coursed up his biceps as a flush of pink scaled down her face and neck. He pressed the head of his achy, engorged flesh to her entrance, easing inside slow enough to savor every inch of her heat. Although he filled her, he'd never been so whole in his life as he reached the hilt.

He blanketed her body with his, rocking with the rate of her breaths and her grip on his ass. Every thrust took him deeper, to a seamless rhythm of heavenly pressure he could spend forever stroking inside of. He buried his face in her neck, salt melting on his tongue and a melody of breathy moans filling his ears. Legs locked around his waist, palms slid up his back, and fingers dug into his shoulders as her walls tightened.

All his senses melded into touch and he rode the surge for as long as he could, tortuously so, until she pulsed around him, and he let the fire ignite.

人

Forrest awoke to a cool sea breeze coming through the open French doors. Patience stood on the balcony off their bedroom in the still of the night beneath a massive, electric-white moon, wrapped inside his coat.

Across the country, the same moon shone high above snow-covered spruces older than Forrest, across sweating mountains and melting glaciers. Time preyed on them all like grizzlies on salmon, threatening to run the rivers dry and the oceans black, to shake the earth until man fell with it.

Alaska was in desperate need of change, and they would make it happen. They had to.

"Patience?"

She spun around to him. "You must be freezing. I'm sorry."

"I'm fine." He stepped out onto the balcony with his arms extended, the sea snoring quietly along the beach. "I need to ask you something."

She crossed the wooden planks and curled into his chest. "Alaska."

He held her, chuckling. "You want to go back?"

"Absolutely."

"There's something you need to know." He brushed her hair away with his fingers, her eyes welcoming every word he had to say. "Locke Industries...it's ours if we want it."

Decisions couldn't be solely his anymore, even if he knew exactly what he wanted to do. There were two vastly different lives he had to offer Patience, and one of them came with the best version of himself.

She pressed her palm against his chest. "What are you talking about?"

"The FBI discovered my shares were never sold when I left the company." He should have known it was all going to come back to him. "My mother forged the transaction as a property sale of some underdeveloped land in Kodiak."

He was a savior of sorts, but not the one Locke Industries needed him to be.

"Why would she do that?" Patience frowned, gaze turning toward the tide.

"She's the one who built Locke Industries. It's her legacy." He understood now more than ever. "She knew what my father and brother would do to it."

Patience grasped the balcony railing, her poker-face coming and going. "What are you going to do?"

"That's what I have to ask you about." He grabbed both of her hands, caught off guard by his own vulnerability as the question played over and over in his mind. "I want to be an Alaska State Trooper for the rest of my life, and I need to know if you're okay with that."

She raised their intertwined fingers to her lips, head falling to the side. "Forrest..."

"There'll be hard days, rough nights, and not a lot of money." He let the flood gates open. "But it's how I make a difference, and it's the only way I know how to protect you while you do the same thing."

She put their hands over his heart. "It's who you are, Forrest. I know that."

"I know I can get tangled up in it." He sucked in a gulp of air. "I know I'm not easy to deal with, and I'm throwing away a huge opportunity, but I want you to see everything else I can be."

She held his face, the light in her eyes, unlike anything he had ever seen before. "I do, too, Forrest."

He crushed her in his arms, hugging her with all he had as they swayed beneath the stars. Love wound around his soul as he held his little family, and they held him back.

"Besides," Patience's lips grazed his ear, "Uniform looks good on you, Trooper Locke."

About the Author

Margaret Frank wrote her first story—a spooky tale about a monster in the school library—when she was 8 years old. In high school, she couldn't be found without a romance novel in hand. One college summer, she set out to write a novel of her own. It'll never see the light of day, but it changed her life forever.

Today, Margaret resides in the Carolinas with her husband and children. When she isn't writing you can find her at the beach, making a mess in the kitchen or DIYing her next project. Red wine, chocolate, and coffee are just a few of her favorite things. She loves learning and seeks to understand just about everything.